Rock 'n' Pop Music Trivia

A mind-bending collection of over 1000
fascinating facts, information and
quirky details about pop music and pop stars

Jim Green

WISE PUBLICATIONS
part of The Music Sales Group

London / New York / Paris / Sydney / Copenhagen / Berlin / Madrid / Tokyo

Contents

Chapter 7
Music Festivals

*Facts and figures about
the world's biggest and best
popular music festivals.*

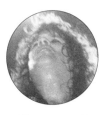

Chapter 5
Artist Trivia

*The reasons behind a band's
name, who has made guest
appearances on other artists
records, what jobs did pop stars
do before they were famous.*

Chapter 8
Sound & Recording

How it all came about…

Chapter 6
Song Lists

*Lists of all the Christmas
number 1s, which records have
been banned, the best movie
songs and the rudest song titles
in the world!*

Chapter 9
Music Genre
Definitions

*What defines Jungle
music and drum 'n' bass?
What are the classic
Prog. Rock albums that
define the genre?*

Published by
Wise Publications
8/9 Frith Street, London W1D 3JB, England.

Exclusive Distributors:
Music Sales Limited
Distribution Centre, Newmarket Road,
Bury St. Edmunds, Suffolk IP33 3YB, England.
Music Sales Corporation
257 Park Avenue South, New York, NY10010,
United States of America.
Music Sales Pty Limited
120 Rothschild Avenue, Rosebery, NSW 2018, Australia.

This book © Copyright 2005 Wise Publications,
a division of Music Sales Limited.
Order No.AM980749
ISBN No. 1-84449-643-0

Photographs courtesy of LFI & Rex Features (*John Lennon page 14*).
Illustrated by Andy Hammond.
Printed in China.

Your Guarantee of Quality:
As publishers, we strive to produce every book to
the highest commercial standards.
Throughout, the printing and binding have been planned to
ensure a sturdy, attractive publication which should give years of enjoyment.
If your copy fails to meet our high standards,
please inform us and we will gladly replace it.

www.musicsales.com

Chapter 1
General Trivia

MUSIC TRIVIA TIT-BITS

PAUL McCARTNEY

MOST RECORDED SONG:

'*Yesterday*' written by Paul McCartney is the most recorded song ever, with over 1,600 cover versions made from 1965 onwards, Matt Monro taking it to number 8 in October that year. The song was also a number 8 hit for The Beatles in 1976, but was originally written for Billy J. Kramer who turned it down. Other artists to release a cover of the song include Wet Wet Wet, Ray Charles, Elvis Presley and Frank Sinatra. '*Yesterday*' was also the most played song on American radio for eight years running.

MOST POPULAR NAME FOR A HIT SINGLE:

'*Crazy*' is the most popular title for a hit single. There are 16 entries for a song of this title in the charts, the biggest hits being Seal at number 2 (1990), Mark Morrison at number 6 (1996) and Mud at number 15 (1994).

SEAL

LONGEST TITLE FOR HIT ALBUM:

Fiona Apple holds the record for the longest hit album title. The title is 90 words long, and was released in 1999, reaching number 46 in the US charts: *'When The Pawn Hits The Conflicts He Thinks Like A King What He Knows Throws The Blows When He Goes To The Fight And He'll Win The Whole Thing 'Fore He Enters The Ring There's Nobody To Batter When Your Mind Is Your Might So When You Go Solo You Hold Your Own Hand And Remember That Depth Is The Greatest Of Heights And If You Know Where You Stand Then You Know Where To Land And If You Fall It Won't Matter Cuz You'll Know That You're Right'.*

LONGEST TITLE OF HIT SINGLE:

The Faces hold the record for the longest title of a hit single, with *'You Can Make Me Dance, Sing Or Anything Even Take The Dog For A Walk, Mend A Fuse, Fold Away The Ironing Board Or Any Other Domestic Short Coming'* totalling 114 letters. This song reached number 12 in the UK charts, 1974.

LONGEST ONE WORD HIT ALBUM TITLE:

'Deckandrumsandrockandroll' by the Propellerheads. The album was released in 1998 by Wall Of Sound, and charted at number 6, remaining in the charts for a further 13 weeks.

LONGEST DURATION OF HIT SINGLE IN ROCK HISTORY:

DON McLEAN

The longest hit single is *'American Pie'* by Don McLean which lasts 8 minutes and 32 seconds. The single reached number 2 in 1972 and is a tribute to the late Buddy Holly. A shortened cover version was released in 2000 by Madonna, which hit the number 1 spot in the UK.

LONGEST RUNNING COMPILATION SERIES:

The longest running recorded music compilation series is the *'Now, That's What I Call Music'* series which began in December 1983. Since then the series has accumulated over 75 number 1 compilation albums.

YOUNGEST ARTIST TO HAVE A US NUMBER 1 ALBUM:

Stevie Wonder is the youngest artist to have a number 1 US album, being just 13 when his album *'Little Stevie Wonder – The Twelve Year Old Genius'* topped the charts in 1963.

YOUNGEST ARTIST TO HAVE A UK NUMBER 1 ALBUM:

Neil Reid is the youngest artist to have a UK number 1 album. He was 12 years old when *'Neil Reid'* hit the top spot in 1972. Reid's biggest UK single is *'Mother Of Mine'*, which reached number 2 that same year. The youngest female to have a UK number 1 album is Avril Lavigne, who was 18 years and 4 months old when *'Let Go'* hit the top spot in 2002.

YOUNGEST INTERNATIONAL ARTIST TO HAVE A NUMBER 1 HIT SINGLE:

The youngest singer to make it to number 1 is Little Jimmy Osmond, who had a UK hit with *'Long Haired Lover From Liverpool'* in 1972. He was 9 years and 8 months old.

YOUNGEST BAND TO DEBUT AT NUMBER 1 IN THE UK ALBUM & SINGLES CHART:

British group McFly are the youngest band to have a number 1 album and number 1 single in the UK charts at the same time. The album *'Room On The 3rd Floor'* topped the charts in 2004. The singles *'Five Colours In Her Hair'* and *'Obviously'* also topped the charts in this year.

YOUNGEST BRITISH MALE ARTIST TO HAVE A UK NUMBER 1:

The youngest British male solo artist to make it to the UK number 1 spot is Gareth Gates, who was 17 years and 8 months old when his cover of *'Unchained Melody'* topped the charts in March 2002. He was propelled into stardom after being the runner-up in the first ever British Pop Idol TV talent competition.

YOUNGEST FEMALE ARTIST TO HAVE A UK NUMBER 1:

Helen Shapiro was 14 years and 10 months old when *'You Don't Know'* topped the UK charts in 1961. Teenage popstress Billie (Piper) was a close contender when she hit the top spot in 1998 with *'Girlfriend'* at the age of 15.

JIMMY OSMOND

OLDEST ARTIST TO HAVE A NUMBER 1 HIT:

The oldest singer to have a number 1 hit is Louis Armstrong who was 67 years and 10 months old when he reached number 1 with 'What A Wonderful World' in 1968. Cher is the oldest solo female artist to have a UK number 1 with 'Believe' at the age of 52.

FIRST ARTIST TO HAVE A NUMBER 1 RECORD WHILE IN PRISON:

'Me Against The World' by Tupac Shakur was released while he was in prison. Shakur was the first artist to have a number 1 album whilst serving time.

TUPAC SHAKUR

FIRST BRITISH US CHARTING ACT:

The Tornados were the first British band to top the US Billboard charts with the instrumental classic 'Telstar' in 1962. The song also topped the UK charts that same year.

US – UK CHART CROSS OVER:

Elton John is the only artist to chart every year from 1971-1999 in both the UK and the US and has topped the US chart a record 16 times! He also holds the record for having the biggest-selling single of all time, 'Candle In The Wind 1997', which sold nearly 5 million copies in the UK and over 11 million in the US. The year 2000 was the only year not to have a single release, although his greatest hits album 'One Night Only' reached number 7 in the album charts.

ELTON JOHN

LARGEST EVER PAYING AUDIENCE:

The largest ever paying audience for a rock artist is recorded as being in 1990 at a Paul McCartney gig, at the Maracana Stadium, in Rio De Janeiro, Brazil, where 184,368 people attended.

LARGEST FREE ROCK CONCERT:

The largest recorded free rock concert was held on New Years Eve, 1984, on Copacabana beach, Rio de Janeiro, Brazil by Rod Stewart. The gig attracted an audience of around 3.5 million people.

MOST CONCERTS PERFORMED IN MOST CONTINENTS IN 24 HOURS:

British rock band Def Leppard currently hold the record for this odd feat. On October 23rd 1995, they played in three continents, beginning in Morocco, then to London and finishing in Vancouver at 11.30pm on the same day. Madness.

FIRST NON-ASIAN ACT TO PERFORM IN CHINA:

This was Wham!, in April 1985, when they performed to 10,000 people in Bejing.

WHAM!

CUBA:

The first Western group to play in Cuba for over 20 years were the Manic Street Preachers in 2001. President Fidel Castro considered Western rock music to be a "decadent influence" after the revolution in 1959, and many young Cubans had not heard this style of music before. Castro was a surprise guest of honour at the sold out gig in Havana.

JERRY GARCIA

MOST VALUABLE GUITAR:

In 2002 an anonymous bidder paid £583,992 for Jerry Garcia's (late guitarist of the Grateful Dead) 'Tiger' guitar. Built by guitar maker Doug Irwin, and taking six years to make, Garcia played 'Tiger' for 11 years. Garcia had left his guitar to Irwin in his will.

MOST VALUABLE JAZZ INSTRUMENT:

The most valuable jazz instrument in the world to date is Charlie Parker's saxophone, which sold for £93,500 at a Christie's auction in 1994.

General Trivia

JOHN LENNON

MOST VALUABLE PIECE OF POP MEMORABILIA:

The most valuable piece of pop memorabilia is John Lennon's Phantom V Rolls Royce car, which sold for a massive $2,229,000 in 1985. Lennon first owned the car in 1965.

CHARLIE PARKER

PAUL & LINDA McCARTNEY (WINGS)

General Trivia

RICHEST POP STAR IN THE WORLD:

This title goes to Sir Paul McCartney, who has become the world's first pop star billionaire. The release of the 2000 Beatles compilation album *I* pushed McCartney's earnings over the billion mark. David Bowie is next on the rich list, reported to have a fortune of £510 million.

RICHEST PERSON IN POP

Beating Paul McCartney in 2004, Clive Calder gets this title. He launched Zomba Records in 1971, and then sold to BMG in 2002 for a reported £1,235 billion.

Chapter 2
Best Sellers

BEST SELLING ALBUMS IN THE WORLD

1. THRILLER – MICHAEL JACKSON

Copies sold: 47 million +

Released: 1982

Produced by Quincy Jones, this album was an enormous success, resulting in seven top 10 singles in the US, as well as receiving eight Grammy awards. In 'Thriller' Michael Jackson produced a style of music that heavily influenced the future of dance music. Jackson never quite got over the success of the album that made him a global superstar, and it proved an impossible feat for him to improve on this epic work.

2. THEIR GREATEST HITS – EAGLES

Copies sold: 31 million +

Released: 1976

3. SATURDAY NIGHT FEVER – VARIOUS ARTISTS (SOUNDTRACK)

Copies sold: 30 million +

Released: 1977

This is the best selling soundtrack of all time, selling over 30 million copies, with most of the songs written and recorded by The Bee Gees. It scored 10 separate chart hits in the US and UK, six of which hit the number 1 spot.

JOHN TRAVOLTA

4. COME ON OVER – SHANIA TWAIN

Copies sold: 30 million +
Released: 1998
*This album is the best selling country album of all time. Twain is
one of the few country artists who has managed to cross over into
the pop charts in both the UK and the US.*

5. JAGGED LITTLE PILL – ALANIS MORISSETTE

Copies sold: 29 million +
Released: 1995
*Alanis Morissette was the first female Canadian artist to score
a US number 1 album. The album was also a huge success in the UK,
reaching number 1 in 1995 and totalling a mammoth 172 weeks in
the album chart.*

6. RUMOURS – FLEETWOOD MAC

Copies sold: 26 million +
Released: 1977

7. FOUR SYMBOLS (LED ZEPPELIN 4) – LED ZEPPELIN

Copies sold: 26 million +
Released: 1971

8. BAT OUT OF HELL – MEATLOAF

Copies sold: 24 million +
Released: 1978

9. DARK SIDE OF THE MOON – PINK FLOYD

Copies sold: 23 million +
Released: 1973
*This album remained
in the top 100 for
over 10 years and
remains to be
the best selling
concept album.*

PINK FLOYD

10. *I* – THE BEATLES
Copies sold: 23 million +
Released: 2000

This album is the fastest selling album of all time (world-wide), and also the first official collection of all the number Is by the British band.

THE EAGLES

11. *HOTEL CALIFORNIA* – THE EAGLES
Copies sold: 23 million +
Released: 1976

12. *BACK IN BLACK* – AC/DC
Copies sold: 23 million +
Released: 1980

AC/DC

MARK KNOPFLER
(DIRE STRAITS)

1. SGT. PEPPER'S LONELY HEARTS CLUB BAND – THE BEATLES

Copies sold: 4.5 million +

Released: 1967

Part of the success of this album was down to the timing of its release. The summer of 1967 was a peak time for sex, drugs and rock 'n' roll, and this album was perfect to match that feeling. The album cover was designed by Peter Blake, and is one of the most famous album covers of all time.

2. (WHAT'S THE STORY) MORNING GLORY – OASIS

Copies sold: 4.2 million +

Released: 1995

Released at the height of the Brit-Pop movement, the album reached number 1, and stayed in the charts for a total of 145 weeks.

3. BROTHERS IN ARMS – DIRE STRAITS

Copies sold: 3.9 million +

Released: 1985

3. BAD – MICHAEL JACKSON

Copies sold: 3.9 million +

Released: 1987

5. *THE IMMACULATE COLLECTION* – **MADONNA**
Copies sold: 3.6 million +
Released: 1990

5. *ABBA GOLD GREATEST HITS* – **ABBA**
Copies sold: 3.6 million +
Released: 1992

7. *STARS* – SIMPLY RED
Copies sold: 3.6 million +
Released: 1991

SIMPLY RED

8. *THRILLER* – **MICHAEL JACKSON**
Copies sold: 3.3 million +
Released: 1982

8. *GREATEST HITS (VOLUME 1)* – **QUEEN**
Copies sold: 3.3 million +
Released: 1981
This album holds the record for spending the most number of weeks in the album charts, 531 weeks in total.

10. *SPICE* – **SPICE GIRLS**
Copies sold: 3.0 million +
Released: 1996

10. *RUMOURS* – **FLEETWOOD MAC**
Copies sold: 3.0 million +
Released: 1977

10. *JAGGED LITTLE PILL* – **ALANIS MORISSETTE**
Copies sold: 3.0 million +
Released: 1995

10. *COME ON OVER* – **SHANIA TWAIN**
Copies sold: 3.0 million +
Released: 1998

BEST SELLING SINGLES OF ALL TIME

1. 'CANDLE IN THE WIND (1997)' – ELTON JOHN

Copies sold: 37 million +
Released: 1994

The song was performed by Elton John at the funeral of Diana Princess of Wales (1997) resulting in a number 1 in almost every country. In the UK alone, the record sold almost five million copies in six weeks. Originally released in 1974, the song peaked at number 11 in the British charts, and was a tribute to Marilyn Monroe. Elton John has said he will never perform the 'Diana' version of the song again.

ELTON JOHN

2. 'WHITE CHRISTMAS' – BING CROSBY

Copies sold: 30 million +
Released: 1943

Written by Irving Berlin, and originally featured in the 1942 movie Holiday Inn starring Crosby and Fred Astaire, 'White Christmas' is the best selling Christmas single of all time.

3. 'ROCK AROUND THE CLOCK' – BILL HALEY & THE COMETS

Copies sold: 17 million +
Released: 1954

4. 'I WANT TO HOLD YOUR HAND' – THE BEATLES

Copies sold: 12 million +
Released: 1963

5. *'HEY JUDE'* – THE BEATLES
Copies sold: 10 million +
Released: 1968

5. *'IT'S NOW OR NEVER'* – ELVIS PRESLEY
Copies sold: 10 million +
Released: 1960

5. *'I WILL ALWAYS LOVE YOU'* – WHITNEY HOUSTON
Copies sold: 10 million +
Released: 1993

Originally written and recorded by Dolly Parton in 1975, this song was a huge hit for Whitney Houston owing to the success of the film The Bodyguard *for which it was the theme song.*

8. *'HOUND DOG'/ 'DON'T BE CRUEL'* – ELVIS PRESLEY
Copies sold: 9 million +
Released: 1956

8. *'DIANA'* – PAUL ANKA
Copies sold: 9 million +
Released: 1957

10. *'I'M A BELIEVER'* – THE MONKEES
Copies sold: 8 million +
Released: 1966

10. *'(EVERYTHING I DO) I DO IT FOR YOU'* – BRYAN ADAMS
Copies sold: 8 million +
Released: 1991

The theme song to the block-buster film Robin Hood - Prince Of Thieves.

Best Sellers

PAUL ANKA

ELVIS PRESLEY

EMINEM

RECORD SALES FACTS

FASTEST SELLING ALBUM IN THE WORLD:
The Beatles *1* is the fastest selling album of all time, selling 3.6 million copies worldwide in the first week of its release in November 2000, beating *NSync's *No Strings Attached* which had sold 2.4 million copies in its first week, also in 2000. The album is the first collection of all the number 1s by the British band.

FASTEST SELLING RAP RECORD:
The fastest selling rap record is Eminem's *The Marshall Mathers EP* which sold 1.76 million copies in its first week of release.

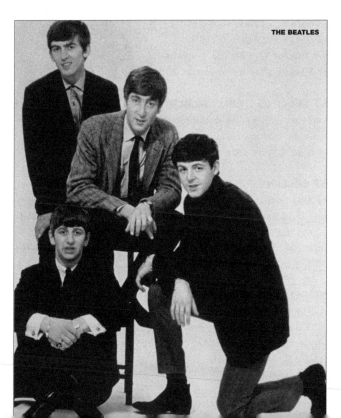

THE BEATLES

FASTEST SELLING ALBUM BY A FEMALE ARTIST:

Britney Spears holds the record for having the fastest selling album by a female artist, in June 2000 with *Oops!... I Did It Again*, which sold 1.3 million copies in its first week in the US alone.

FASTEST SELLING ALBUM IN THE UK:

Be Here Now by Oasis reached the 1 million record sales mark just 17 days after its release in 1997. The Beatles *1* comes a close second, hitting 1 million record sales in 26 days.

FASTEST SELLING ALBUM IN UK BY SOLO MALE ARTIST:

Robbie Williams's *Swing When You're Winning* (2000) sold 1 million records in just 29 days.

FASTEST SELLING ALBUM IN UK BY SOLO FEMALE ARTIST:

Dido's *Life For Rent* hit the 1 million point 50 days after its release in 2003.

DIDO

BEST SELLING DEBUT ALBUM:

The world's best selling debut album is *Boston* by Boston, released in 1976 and has sold more than 16 million copies.

BEST SELLING RAP/HIP-HOP ALBUM IN THE US:

Crazy Sexy Cool by TLC is the best selling rap/hip-hop album in the US, selling over 11 million copies since its release in 1994, with help from the number 1 hit singles 'Waterfalls' and 'Creep'. In April 2002 Lisa 'Left Eye' Lopes – the group's rapper – was killed in a car crash in Honduras at the age of 30.

BEST SELLING REGGAE ALBUM:

Legend by Bob Marley is the best selling reggae album with over 11.8 million copies sold worldwide since 1984. The album is a collection of 15 of Marley's hits and managed to stay in the UK chart for a massive 106 weeks.

BEST SELLING WORLD MUSIC ALBUM:

The best selling world music album is *Buena Vista Social Club* which has sold in excess of 4 million copies worldwide. In 1996 Rye Cooder gathered together some of Cuba's greatest musicians to collaborate on this award winning album.

BEST SELLING LATIN MALE ARTIST:

The best selling Latin male artist is Julio Iglesias who has sold over 200 million albums worldwide since his debut in 1981. *Julio* (1987) was the first foreign language album to sell more than 2 million copies in the US. Enrique Iglesias, Julio's son, is the currently the biggest selling Spanish language artist in the world.

BEST SELLING LATIN FEMALE ARTIST:

This title goes to Gloria Estefan, who has sold over 35 million records worldwide. In 1990 Estefan was awarded a Golden Globe for her album sales outside the USA.

BEST SELLING FUNK ALBUM:

Jamiroquai's 1996 *Travelling Without Moving* is the best selling funk album of all time, with over 7 million copies sold worldwide. *'Virtual Insanity'*, a hit single from the album, won the band a Grammy for best pop performance in February 1998.

BEST SELLING DRUM 'N' BASS ALBUM:

The best selling drum 'n' bass album is *New Forms* by Roni Size & Reprazent, which has sold over 700,000 copies since its release in 1997. This album won the band the 1997 Mercury Music award for best album of the year.

BEST SELLING BIG BEAT ALBUM:

You've Come A Long Way Baby by Fatboy Slim is the world's best selling big beat album, with sales of over 3 million copies sold, 1 million of those in the UK alone. Released in 1998 the album contains the number 1 hit *'Praise You'*, and the number 2 hit *'Right Here Right Now'*.

BEST ALL TIME BAND SALES
IN THE WORLD:

The Beatles have amassed the greatest number of record sales beating every other act, with over one billion records sold worldwide since their debut single *'Please Please Me'* in 1963.

BEST SELLING SINGLE BY
A FEMALE GROUP:

The best selling single by a female group is *'Wannabe'* by the Spice Girls, which was released in July 1996. It hit the top spot in 32 countries, spending 7 weeks at number 1 in the UK. It has sold 1.2 million copies worldwide.

FIRST SONG TO TOP UK CHARTS
FOUR TIMES:

The song *'Unchained Melody'* is the first song to top the UK charts on four occasions: Jimmy Young (1955), The Righteous Brothers (1990 – re-released for the film *Ghost*; on first release it only went to number 14), Robson & Jerome (1995) and Gareth Gates (2002). The tune however was originally an instrumental composed by Alex North, for the film *Unchained*, then Hy Zaret wrote lyrics for it.

SINGLE MOST WEEKS ON CHART:

'My Way' by Frank Sinatra is the song that has spent the longest on the singles chart, with 124 weeks in total. The song has been covered by a range of artists including Dorothy Squires, Elvis Presley, Sex Pistols (sung by Sid Vicious) and Shane MacGowan.

LONGEST TIME SPENT ON ALBUM CHARTS:

The Beatles have spent the longest time in total on the album charts, amassing a mammoth 1292 weeks. Queen are in second place having spent a total of 1271 weeks, and Elvis Presley in third place with a total of 1267 weeks. Madonna is the only female solo artist to accumulate over 1000 weeks, knocking up a total of 1051, and coming in at number 7 of total album sales, behind Dire Straits, Simon & Garfunkel and U2.

Best Sellers

THE SPICE GIRLS

NUMBER 1 SINGLE TO SPEND MOST CONSECUTIVE WEEKS IN CHARTS:

'I Believe' by Frankie Laine with Paul Weston and his Orchestra is the single that has spent most consecutive weeks at number 1; 18 weeks in total in 1953. Bryan Adams' *'(Everything I Do) I Do It For You'* closely follows with 16 weeks (1991), and *'Love Is All Around'* by Wet Wet Wet is in third position with 15 weeks (1994), helped by being on the soundtrack to the popular British film *Four Weddings And A Funeral*.

ARTIST SPENDING MOST WEEKS ON CHART:

In total, Elvis Presley has spent the most weeks on the chart, accumulating 1193 weeks, closely followed by Cliff Richard who has amassed 1154 weeks. These two artists almost double number three on the list, which is Elton John, who has spent a total of 614 weeks on the chart.

ARTIST WITH MOST HIT SINGLES:

Bing Crosby had a total of 156 hits between 1931 and 1940. He recorded an estimated 2,600 songs in his career, and had 317 successful records before the birth of rock 'n' roll and the official charts. Since the charts began in 1952, Cliff Richard holds the record for having the most hit singles, with a total of 125, 10 hits more than Elvis, who has had 115 hits. With Sony/BMG re-releasing all of Presley's original UK number 1 singles to commemorate Elvis' 70th birthday year, Cliff Richard could soon lose this hard-earned title.

BING CROSBY

ARTIST WITH MOST TOP 10 SINGLES:

Cliff Richard also holds the record for having most top 10 singles with a monstrous 65 songs. Elvis Presley closely follows in second position with 58 songs, and Madonna comes in third with 53 songs.

ARTIST WITH MOST NUMBER 1 SINGLES:

Elvis Presley has had the most number 1 singles, a total of 18. The Beatles are right behind him with 17 number 1s, and Cliff Richard behind them with 14. Presley's tally keeps on rising with the re-release of all 18 singles during what would have been his 70th birthday year, 2005.

MOST NUMBER 1 ALBUMS:

The Beatles have had the most number 1 albums, 15 in total. Elvis Presley and The Rolling Stones both have had 10 number 1s.

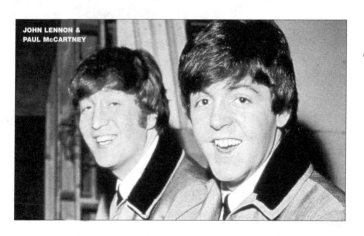

JOHN LENNON & PAUL McCARTNEY

SONGWRITER TO WRITE MOST NUMBER 1s:

John Lennon just pips Paul McCartney to the post by holding the title of most number 1s written, with 29 songs; McCartney has 28. In third position are ABBA's Benny Andersson and Björn Ulvaeus who have written 12 number 1 singles. Spice Girls' Melanie C is at number four in this list, with credits for 11 number 1 singles under her belt, nine of those being with the Spice Girls.

ARTIST TO HAVE MOST NUMBER 2 SINGLES:
Madonna has had the most number 2 singles, 11 in total, closely followed by Kylie Minogue and Cliff Richard who both have had 10.

PRODUCER OF MOST NUMBER 1s:
George Martin (producer of The Beatles) has produced the largest number of number 1s, 28 in total.

POSTHUMOUS NUMBER 1 SINGLE:
Elvis Presley has had the longest gap between his death and a number 1 single, with a re-issue of 'It's Now Or Never' in 2005, hitting the top spot 27 years after his death in 1977.

BUDDY HOLLY

POSTHUMOUS NUMBER 1 ALBUM:
Buddy Holly has had the longest gap between his death and a number 1 album, with 'Words Of Love' reaching the number 1 spot in 1993, 34 years, 2 weeks and 3 days after his death in 1959. Eva Cassidy has had three number 1 posthumous albums after her death in 1996, with Songbird, Imagine, and American Tune.

MOST POSTHUMOUS NUMBER I SINGLES:

Elvis Presley now holds the record for having the most posthumous number I singles. 'Way Down' was his first, released 17 days after his death in 1977, then followed by the JXL remix of 'A Little Less Conversation' in 2002. More recently in 2005, re-issues of 'Jailhouse Rock', 'One Night/I Got Stung' and 'It's Now Or Never' have also reached number I. John Lennon has had three posthumous number Is with '(Just Like) Starting Over', 'Imagine' and 'Woman'. Buddy Holly, Eddie Cochran, Jim Reeves, Jimi Hendrix, Jackie Wilson, Freddie Mercury, Aaliyah and George Harrison have all had one posthumous number I single.

ARTIST WITH MOST CONSECUTIVE NUMBER I ALBUMS:

Led Zeppelin have had eight consecutive number I albums, *Led Zeppelin II* (first charted in 1969), *Led Zeppelin 3* (1970), *Four Symbols (Led Zeppelin 4)** (1971), *Houses Of The Holy* (1973), *Physical Graffiti* (1975), *Presence* (1976), *The Song Remains The Same* (1976) and *In Through The Out Door* (1979).

*Four Symbols (Led Zeppelin 4) was originally untitled, but is commonly referred to as either of these titles. ABBA have also had eight consecutive number I albums, although three of these are greatest hits/singles collections.

FIRST SINGLE TO TOP US & UK CHARTS SIMULTANEOUSLY

The first single to hit the number I spot in the US and the UK at the same time is Hanson's *'Mmmbop'* in June 1997. The band was made up of three brothers the youngest – Zac – being just 12 when the single reached number I.

HANSON

Chapter 3
Chart History

JIMMY SAVILLE ON *TOP OF THE POPS*

UK SINGLES CHARTS HISTORY

The first UK Singles Chart began in 1952, when a Top 12 was compiled based on sales that various UK record stores sent in to the NME journal. In 1956 this became the Top 20.

From 1960 to 1969 the official UK charts were produced by combining the charts of the country's four main music magazines: Record Mirror, Melody Maker, New Musical Express, Dic & Music Echo.

After the launch of BBC Radio 1 on September 30th 1967, the singles chart became the BBC Top 30, with a rundown of the Top 20 every Sunday afternoon.

To eradicate any form of 'chart fixing' by unscrupulous promoters who had tendencies to buy records in bulk in order to increase chart positions, a new, computerised method was introduced in 1969.

From 1983 the charts were compiled with the aid of the market research agency GALLUP.

From 1998 the charts were managed by the Official UK Charts Company. On 17th April 2005, the Official Singles Chart integrated digital downloads alongside physical singles to create the chart.

THE RECORD INDUSTRY ASSOCIATION OF AMERICA AWARDS

Launched in 1958, the RIAA Awards are the longest-running measure of achievement for sound recordings in the USA. Each year artists are presented with certificates to mark the success of their records. The figures are based on retail, mail order and record club sales, promotional copies are not included.

THE RIAA AWARDS

Gold Award 500,000 copies sold

Platinum Award 1,000,000 copies sold

Multiplatinum Award 2,000,000 copies sold

Diamond Award 10,000,000 + copies sold

AWARD FACTS

The RIAA awarded the very first Gold plaque to Perry Como on March 14th 1958, for the hit single, 'Catch A Falling Star'.

The first Gold album was awarded to *Oklahoma* sung by Gordon Macrae and the original cast, also in 1958.

PERRY COMO

The first platinum single was awarded to Johnny Taylor for 'Disco Lady'.

The first Platinum album was The Eagles' *Their Greatest Hits 1971-1975*.

Elvis Presley currently holds the most RIAA certificates by a single artist, with 235 awards in total: 132 Gold, 70 Platinum and 33 multi-platinum.

The first Diamond Awards were launched in 1999. These honour artists and bands who have released albums or singles that have sold 10 million or more units.

The Beatles have earned an unprecedented six diamond awards for their albums, *1*, *Sgt. Peppers Lonely Hearts Club Band*, *Abbey Road*, *The Beatles*, *The Beatles 1962-1966* and *The Beatles 1967-1970*.

Chapter 4
Awards

A GRAMMY AWARD

THE GRAMMYS

The Grammy Awards, set up in 1958, are considered to be the most coveted music industry awards in the world. There are a total of 105 award categories which cover all musical styles. Here are highlights of the 2005 awards:

RECORD OF THE YEAR
Ray Charles & Norah Jones
'Here We Go Again'

ALBUM OF THE YEAR
Ray Charles, *Genius Loves Company*

BEST NEW ARTIST
Maroon 5

Awards

BEST SONG
John Mayer, *'Daughters'*

BEST ROCK SONG
U2, *'Vertigo'*

BEST ROCK ALBUM
Green Day, *American Idiot*

BEST ALTERNATIVE ROCK ALBUM
Wilco, *A Ghost Is Born*

RAY CHARLES

BEST R 'N' B ALBUM
Alicia Keys, *The Diary Of Alicia Keys*

BEST DANCE RECORDING
Britney Spears, *'Toxic'*

TRADITIONAL POP VOCAL ALBUM
Rod Stewart, *Stardust... The Great
American Songbook Volume III*

BEST RAP SONG
Kanye West, *'Jesus Walks'*

BEST RAP ALBUM
Kanye West, *The College Dropout*

**BEST SHORT FORM
MUSIC VIDEO**
U2 *'Vertigo'*

BEST LONG FORM MUSIC VIDEO
Sam Cooke *'Legend'*

KANYE WEST

*At the very first Grammy Awards in 1958,
the key winners were:*

ALBUM OF THE YEAR
Henry Mancini *The Music From Peter Gunn*

BEST VOCAL PERFORMANCE, FEMALE
Ella Fitzgerald *'Ella Fitzgerald Sings The Irving
Berlin Songbook'*

BEST VOCAL PERFORMANCE, MALE
Perry Como *'Catch A Falling Star'*

BEST PERFORMANCE BY A DANCE BAND
Count Basie *'Basie'*

BEST PERFORMANCE BY A VOCAL GROUP
Keely Smith & Louis Prima *'That Old Black Magic'*

BEST RHYTHM & BLUES PERFORMANCE
The Champs *'Tequila'*

THE LEGEND AWARDS

In 1990 the Legend Awards were set up to award individuals or groups for their contributions and influence in the recording industry, although the awards are not presented every year. The list of winners is listed below:

1990 Andrew Lloyd Webber/Liza Minnelli/Willie Nelson/ Smokey Robinson

1991 Johnny Cash/Aretha Franklin/ Billy Joel/Quincy Jones

1992 Barbra Streisand

1993 Michael Jackson

1994 Curtis Mayfield/Frank Sinatra

1998 Luciano Pavarotti

1999 Elton John

2003 Bee Gees

JOHNNY CASH

HALL OF FAME AWARDS – SINGLES

The Grammy Hall Of Fame Award was established in 1973 to honour recordings that have made a lasting impact on music. The song must be at least 25 years old. Songs in the list include: 'Your Song' (Elton John), 'Layla' (Derek & The Dominos), 'Walk On By' (Dionne Warwick), 'House Of The Rising Sun' (The Animals), 'Imagine' (John Lennon & The Plastic Ono Band), 'I Want You Back' (Jackson 5), 'Lady Marmalade' (LaBelle), 'My Way' (Frank Sinatra),

'Moon River' (Henry Mancini), 'Hotel California' (The Eagles) and 'Stairway To Heaven' (Led Zeppelin).

Both The Beatles and Elvis Presley have five songs in the list; Ray Charles, Bob Dylan and Marvin Gaye have four and Chuck Berry, Aretha Franklin, Roy Orbison, Little Richard, The Supremes and Stevie Wonder all have three.

UK MUSIC HALL OF FAME

In 2004 the UK held its first UK Music Hall Of Fame awards which were split into decade categories. A shortlist of 10 artists were decided upon by industry experts, and the final award decisions were left to a public vote. Five 'founder' members were automatically included in the awards – Madonna, Elvis Presley, Bob Marley, U2 and The Beatles. The other winners were Cliff Richard (for the 1950s), The Rolling Stones (60s), Queen (70s), Michael Jackson (80s) and Robbie Williams (90s). The winners were inaugurated into the UK Music Hall Of Fame in November 2004 which was aired by Channel 4.

BOB MARLEY

THE BRIT AWARDS

Originally called The Britannia awards in 1977, the ceremony was created to celebrate 100 years of recorded sound, and to honour the best acts in popular music over the last 25 years. In 1989 it was renamed the Brit Awards. Winners of the 1977 awards were:

BEST BRITISH MALE SOLO ARTIST
Cliff Richard

BEST BRITISH FEMALE SOLO ARTIST
Shirley Bassey

BEST BRITISH GROUP
The Beatles

BEST BRITISH ALBUM
The Beatles, *Sgt Pepper's Lonely Heart Club Band*

BEST BRITISH NEWCOMER
Julie Covington

BEST BRITISH SINGLE
Queen, 'Bohemian Rhapsody'

OUTSTANDING CONTRIBUTION
L.G. Wood/The Beatles (joint winners)

BEST BRITISH PRODUCER
George Martin

BEST INTERNATIONAL SINGLE
Simon & Garfunkel, 'Bridge Over Troubled Water'

BEST INTERNATIONAL ALBUM
Simon & Garfunkel, *Bridge Over Troubled Water*

Awards

SHIRLEY BASSEY

FRANZ FERDINAND

BEST ORCHESTRAL ALBUM
Benjamin Britten, *War Requiem*

BEST CLASSICAL SOLOIST ALBUM
Jacqueline Du Pre, *Elgar/Cello Concerto*

BEST BRITISH NON MUSICAL RECORD
Richard Burton & Cast, *Under Milkwood*

In 2005 the Brit Award winners were:

BRITS 25 THE BEST SONG AWARD
Robbie Williams, 'Angels'

BEST BRITISH MALE SOLO ARTIST
The Streets

BEST BRITISH FEMALE SOLO ARTIST
Joss Stone

BEST BRITISH GROUP
Franz Ferdinand

BEST BRITISH ALBUM
Keane, *Hopes And Fears*

BEST BRITISH SINGLE
Will Young, 'Your Game'

BEST BRITISH ROCK ACT
Franz Ferdinand

BEST BRITISH URBAN ACT
Joss Stone

BEST BRITISH LIVE ACT
Muse

JOSS STONE

BRITISH BREAKTHROUGH ARTIST
Keane

52 **BEST POP ACT**
McFly

BEST INTERNATIONAL MALE SOLO ARTIST
Eminem

BEST INTERNATIONAL FEMALE SOLO ARTIST
Gwen Stefani

BEST INTERNATIONAL ALBUM
Scissor Sisters, *Scissor Sisters*

BEST INTERNATIONAL GROUP
Scissor Sisters

INTERNATIONAL BREAKTHROUGH ARTIST
Scissor Sisters

OUTSTANDING CONTRIBUTION TO MUSIC
Sir Bob Geldof

Awards

SIR BOB GELDOF

SCISSOR SISTERS

P. J. HARVEY

MERCURY MUSIC PRIZE

The annual Mercury Music Prize was set up in 1992 to celebrate
UK music as an alternative to the Brit Awards. Each year 12 albums
are selected spanning all musical genres. Originally the prize was
sponsored by the now defunct Mercury telecoms company.
Winners of the awards have been:

1992 Primal Scream – *Screamadelica*

1993 Suede – *Suede*

1994 M People – *Elegant Slumming*

1995 Portishead – *Dummy*

1996 Pulp – *Different Class*

1997 Roni Size/Reprazent – *New Forms*

1998 Gomez – *Bring It On*

1999 Talvin Singh – *OK*

2000 Badly Drawn Boy – *The Hour
Of Bewilderbeast*

2001 P.J. Harvey – *Stories From
The City, Stories From The Sea*

2002 Ms Dynamite –
A Little Deeper

2003 Dizzee Rascal –
Boy In Da Corner

2004 Franz Ferdinand –
Franz Ferdinand

SUEDE

THE MOBO AWARDS

The MOBO (Music Of Black Origin) award ceremony began in 1996 to acknowledge urban music, primarily music which is drawn from the 'black experience', encompassing R & B, Hip Hop, Reggae, Rap, Jazz, Gospel, Garage and World music.

BEST R 'N' B ACTS

1996 Mark Morrison

1997 Shola Ama

1998 Beverley Knight

1999 Beverley Knight

2000 Craig David

2001 Usher

2002 Ashanti

2003 Justin Timberlake

2004 Usher

CRAIG DAVID

BEST HIP HOP ACTS

1996 Blak Twang

1997 Funky DL

1998 Phoebe 1

1999 Roots Manuva

2000 Eminem

2001 Missy Elliott

2002 Ja Rule

2003 50 Cent

2004 Kayne West

MISSY ELLIOTT

Awards

BEST JAZZ ACTS

1996 Courtney Pine

1997 Sunship

1998 Jazz Steppers

1999 Denys Baptiste

2000 Ronnie Jordan
feat. Mos Def

2001 Incognito

2002 Norah Jones

2003 Soweto Kinch

2004 Jamie Cullum

COURTNEY PINE

Q AWARDS

The Q awards started out in 1990 as an opportunity for Q magazine readers to vote for what they thought to be the best music of the previous year.

Q BEST ALBUM AWARD WINNERS

1990 World Party *Goodbye Jumbo*

1991 R.E.M. *Out Of Time*

1992 R.E.M. *Automatic For The People*

1993 Sting *Ten Summoner's Tales*

1994 Blur *Parklife*

1995 Blur *The Great Escape*

1996 Manic Street Preachers
Everything Must Go

1997 Radiohead
OK Computer

1998 Massive Attack
Mezzanine

1999 Chemical Brothers
Surrender

2000 Coldplay *Parachutes*

2001 Travis *The Invisible Band*

2002 Coldplay *A Rush Of Blood To The Head*

2003 Blur *Thinktank*

2004 Keane *Hopes And Fears*

R.E.M.

Awards

Q BEST ACT IN THE WORLD TODAY WINNERS

1990 U2

1991 R.E.M. & U2

1992 U2

1993 U2

1994 R.E.M.

1995 R.E.M.

1996 Oasis

1997 Oasis

1998 Manic Street Preachers

1999 Blur

U2

2000 Travis

2001 Radiohead

2002 Radiohead

2003 Radiohead

2004 Red Hot Chili
Peppers

Q BEST LIVE ACT AWARD WINNERS

1990 The Rolling Stones

1991 Simple Minds

1992 Crowded House

1993 Neil Young

1994 Pink Floyd

1995 Oasis

1996 Pulp

1997 The Prodigy

1998 Roni Size/Reprazent

1999 Stereophonics

2000 Oasis

2001 The Manic Street
Preachers

2002 The Hives

2003 Robbie Williams

2004 Muse

MANIC STREET PREACHERS

*The Eurovision Song Contest began life as the Italian San Remo
Song Festival, and was the brainchild of Frenchman Marcel Baison,
who wanted to unite the nations of post-war Europe. The European
Broadcasting Union began the Eurovision in May 1956 in Switzerland.
Here are the winners, followed by the entry for the United Kingdom.*

Year	Country	Song	UK Entry
1956	Switzerland	'Refrains' Lys Assia	(No UK entry)
1957	Netherlands	'Net Als Toen' Corry Broken	'All' Patricia Bredin
1958	France	'Dors Mon Amour' Andre Claveau	(No UK entry)
1959	Holland	'Een Beetje' Teddy Scholten	'Sing Little Birdie' Pearl Carr & Teddy Johnson
1960	France	'Tom Pillibi' Jacqueline Boyer	'Looking High High High' Bryan Johnson
1961	Luxembourg	'Nous Les Amoureux' Jean Claude Pascal	'Are You Sure' Allisons
1962	France	'Un Premier Amour' Isabelle Aubret	'Ring-A-Ding Girl' Ronnie Carroll
1963	Denmark	'Dansevise' Grethe & Jorgen Ingmann	'Say Wonderful Things' Ronnie Carroll
1964	Italy	'Non Ho L'eta Per Amarti' Gigliola Cinquetti	'I Love The Little Things' Matt Monro
1965	Luxembourg	'Poupee De Cire Poupee De Son' France Gall	'I Belong' Kathy Kirby
1966	Austria	'Merci Cherie' Udo Jurgens	'A Man Without Love' Kenneth Mc.Kellar
1967	UK	'Puppet On A String' Sandie Shaw	'Puppet On A String' Sandie Shaw
1968	Spain	'La La La' Massiel	'Congratulations' Cliff Richard

Awards

SANDIE SHAW

ABBA

Year	Country	Song	UK Entry
1969	(joint)		
	UK	'Boom-Bang-A-Bang' Lulu	'Boom-Bang-A Bang' Lulu
	France	'Un Jour Un Enfant' Frida Boccara	
	Netherlands	'De Troubadour' Lennie Kuhr	
	Spain	'Vivo Cantando' Salome	
1970	Ireland	'All Kinds Of Everything' Dana	'Knock Knock Who's There' Mary Hopkin
1971	Monaco	'Un Banc Un Arbre Un Rue' Severine	'Jack In The Box' Clodagh Rodgers
1972	Luxembourg	'Apres Toi (Come What May)' Vicky Leandros	'Beg Steal Or Borrow' New Seekers
1973	Luxembourg	'Tu Te Reconnaitras (Wonderful Dream)' Ann-Marie David	'Power To All Our Friends' Cliff Richard
1974	Sweden	'Waterloo' Abba	'Long Live Love' Olivia Newton-John
1975	Netherlands	'Ding-A-Dong' Teach-In	'Let Me Be The One' Shadows
1976	UK	'Save Your Kisses For Me' Brotherhood Of Man	'Save Your Kisses For Me' Brotherhood Of Man

BROTHERHOOD OF MAN

Year	Country	Song	UK Entry
1977	France	'L'oiseau et L'enfant' Marie Myriam	'Rock Bottom' Lynsey De Paul & Mike Moran
1978	Israel	'A Ba Ni Bi' Izhar Cohen & Alphabeta	'Bad Old Days' Co-Co
1979	Israel	'Hallelujah' Milk & Honey	'Mary Ann' Black Lace
1980	Ireland	'What's Another Year' Johnny Logan	'Love Enough For Two' Prima Donna

Awards

BUCKS FIZZ

1981	UK	'Making Your Mind Up' Bucks Fizz	'Making Your Mind Up' Bucks Fizz
1982	Germany	'Ein Bisschen Frieden (A Little Peace)' Nicole	'One Step Further' Bardo
1983	Luxembourg	'Si La Vie Est Cadeu' Corrine Hermes	'I'm Never Giving Up' Sweet Dreams
1984	Sweden	'Diggy-Loo Diggy-Ley' Herrys	'Love Games' Belle & The Devotions

Year	Country	Song	UK Entry
1985	Norway	'La Det Swinge (Let It Swing)' Bobbysocks	'Love Is' Vikki
1986	Belgium	'J'aime La Vie' Sandra Kim	'Runner In The Night' Ryder
1987	Ireland	'Hold Me Now' Johnny Logan	'Only The Light' Rikki

CELINE DION

Year	Country	Song	UK Entry
1988	Switzerland	'Ne Partez Sans Moi' Celine Dion	'Go' Scott Fitzgerald
1989	Yugoslavia	'Rock Me' Riva	'Why Do I Always Get It Wrong' Live Report
1990	Italy	'Insieme 1992' Toto Cotugno	'Give A Little Love Back To The World' Emma
1991	Sweden	'Fangad Av En Stormvind' Carola	'A Message To Your Heart' Samantha Janus
1992	Ireland	'Why Me' Linda Martin	'One Step Out Of Time' Michael Ball
1993	Ireland	'In Your Eyes' Naimh Kavanagh	'Better The Devil You Know' Sonia
1994	Ireland	'Rock N Roll Kids' Paul Harrington & Charlie McGettigan	'Lonely Symphony' Francis Ruffelle

Year	Country	Song	UK Entry
1995	Norway	'Nocturne' Secret Garden	'Love City Groove' Love City Groove
1996	Ireland	'The Voice' Eimar Quinn	'Ooh Ah... Just A Little Bit' Gina G

KATRINA & THE WAVES

Awards

Year	Country	Song	UK Entry
1997	UK	'Love Shine A Light' Katrina & The Waves	'Love Shine A Light' Katrina & The Waves
1998	Israel	'Diva' Dana International	'Where Are You' Imaani
1999	Sweden	'Take Me To Your Heaven' Charlotte Nilsson	'Say It Again' Precious
2000	Denmark	'Fly On The Wings Of Love' Olsen Brothers	'Don't Play That Song Again' Nicki French
2001	Estonia	'Everybody' Tanel Badar & Dave Benton	'No Dream Impossible' Lyndsay Dracass
2002	Latvia	'I Wanna' Marie N	'Come Back' Jessica Garlick
2003	Turkey	'Every Way That I Can' Sertab Erener	'Cry Baby' Jemini
2004	Ukraine	'Wild Dances' Ruslana	'Hold On To Our Love' James Fox
2005	Greece	'My Number One' Helen Paparizou	'Touch My Fire' Javine

Chapter 5
Artist Trivia

BAND NAME ORIGINS

*Every band has had to come up with a name that is not only original, but ideally says something about them and their music...
The following list gives the supposed reasons why bands are named as they are.*

APHEX TWIN
The 'Twin' comes from Richard D. James' brother who died before he was born. They shared the same first name, and his memorial stone appears on the cover of the *Boy/Girl* EP. Aphex is a manufacturer of audio equipment, which has been used by Richard D. James

ARAB STRAP
A sexual device; "The classic male potency enhancer..." (as quoted on the packaging)

BLACK SABBATH
A 1963 Boris Karloff classic horror film

CLANNAD
Gaelic for 'family'

DEACON BLUE
From the Steely Dan song 'Deacon's Blues' (from *Aja* (1977))

CLANNAD

EVERYTHING BUT THE GIRL
An East Yorkshire clothing store

THE FOO FIGHTERS
A UFO type object reported by soldiers in WW2

JANE'S ADDICTION
(Allegedly...) A prostitute the band members had all met and who loved them so much, they were literally Jane's addiction!

JETHRO TULL
The inventor of the seed drill, a planting device

KING ADORA
A huge vibrator!

THE KLF
Kopyright Liberation Front

JETHRO TULL

LED ZEPPELIN
Because Keith Moon said that their act would go down like a "lead balloon"

LYNYRD SKYNYRD
After their P.E. teacher, Leonard Skinner, who had given them a hard time in school because of their long hair

MEATLOAF
Nickname given to Marvin Lee Aday after he trod on the toes of his school coach

NEW MODEL ARMY
The name given to Oliver Cromwell's troops in the English Civil War

NIRVANA
The state of perfect blessedness attained through the annihilation of the self (the cycle of reincarnation) (Hindu)

PINK FLOYD
After bluesmen 'Pink' Anderson, and Floyd Council

THE POGUES
From Pogue Mahone, which is Gaelic for 'kiss my arse'

RADIOHEAD
From a Talking Heads song 'Radio Head'
on the *True Stories* album

RADIOHEAD

SIMPLE MINDS
A line from Bowie's 'Jean Genie' ("He's so
simple minded he can't drive his module")

SISTERS OF MERCY
From a Leonard Cohen song of the same
name (from *The Songs Of Leonard Cohen*)

10cc
The metric total of semen ejaculated by the average male,
apparently...

TOTO
Dorothy's dog in *The Wizard Of Oz*

SID VICIOUS
John Lydon named him 'Sid' after his pet hamster, and
'Vicious' after the Lou Reed song

W.A.S.P.
Stands for We Are Sexual Perverts!

LITERARY REFERENCES

*The following bands have taken their name from a book, or some
sort of literary reference:*

THE DOORS
From the *Doors Of Perception* by Aldous Huxley, and a line from
Heaven And Hell by William Blake: "If the doors of perception
were cleansed, everything would appear to man as it is, Infinite"

HEAVEN 17

From a band in the Kubrick film *Clockwork Orange*. The Heaven Seventeen, is the name of one of the groups in the charts when Alex is in the record store

HEAVEN 17

JOY DIVISION

From a book called *House Of Dolls*. In it the Joy Division referred to the wing of Nazi Concentration camps where inmates were used by SS Officers as prostitutes

MOLOKO

The milk bar drink in *Clockwork Orange*

MOTT THE HOOPLE

A character in a novel by Willard Manus

PUBLIC IMAGE LTD.

After Muriel Sparks' novel *The Public Image*

SAVAGE GARDEN

From a passage in the Ann Rice novel *Queen Of The Damned*

STEELY DAN

A metal dildo in *Naked Lunch* by William Burrough

JOHN LYDON (PUBLIC IMAGE LTD.)

STEPPENWOLF

A novel by Herman Hesse about a man who rather surprisingly wanted to be a wolf

SUPERTRAMP

From a W H Davies book *The Autobiography Of A Supertramp*

TEARDROP EXPLODES
A caption from the Marvel comic
Daredevil

TEARS FOR FEARS
From Arthur Janov's book *Prisoners Of Pain*

THOMPSON TWINS
The twin detectives from *Herge's Adventures Of Tin Tin*

TEARS FOR FEARS

URIAH HEEP
A character in Charles Dickens' novel *David Copperfield*

VELVET UNDERGROUND
A soft porn paperback published in the 60s

Artist Trivia

ORIGINAL BAND NAMES

For many reasons, bands decide to change their names into something better and probably more commercial. Here are some of the best changes:

NOW...	WAS...
ABC	Vice Versa
Aerosmith	Chain Reaction
The Alarm	The Toilets
Audioweb	The Sugar Merchants
Bay City Rollers	The Saxons
The Beach Boys	The Pendletones
The Beatles	The Quarrymen
Blondie	Angel & The Snakes
Blur	Seymour
The Boomtown Rats	The Nightlife Thugs

Band	Former Name
The Byrds	The Jet Set/The Beefeaters
Coldplay	Starfish
Creedence Clearwater Revival	The Golliwogs
Crowded House	Split Enz
Culture Club	In Praise Of Lemmings
The Darkness	Empire
Deep Purple	Roundabout
Depeche Mode	Composition Of Sound
Earth, Wind & Fire	The Salty Peppers
Extreme	The Dream
Fairport Convention	Ethnic Shuffle Orchestra
Genesis	Garden Wall
The Grateful Dead	The Warlocks
The Hollies	The Deltas
J. Geils Band	The Hallucinations
Joy Division	Stiff Kittens/Warsaw
The Kinks	The Ravens
Lindisfarne	Downtown Faction
Led Zeppelin	The New Yardbirds
Madness	Invaders
Mötley Crüe	London
Oasis	Rain
Pearl Jam	Mookie Blaylock
Radiohead	On A Friday
Simple Minds	Johnny & The Self Abusers
Simon & Garfunkel	Tom & Jerry
Sonny & Cher	Caesar & Cleo
Supergrass	The Jennifers
The Supremes	The Primettes
The Teardrop Explodes	A Shallow Madness
Teenage Fanclub	The Boy Hairdressers
Temptations	The Neon Boys
10cc	Hotlegs
The Turtles	Nightriders
U2	Feedback/Hype
Wham!	The Executive
The Who	The High Numbers
XTC	The Helium Kidz
ZZ Top	The Moving Sidewalks

MÖTLEY CRÜE

ORIGINAL STAR NAMES

In lots of cases pop stars have changed their original birth name to something they feel suits their pop persona better. Here's a list of some of the more bizarre name changes...

Adam Ant .... Stuart Leslie Goddard
Badly Drawn Boy .... Damon Gough
Captain Beefheart................. Don Van Vliet
Bono... Paul Hewson
Betty Boo .... Alison Clarkson
Chubby Checker .... Earnest Evans
Alice Cooper .... Vincent Furnier
Bo Diddley .... Elias Bates
The Edge .... Dave Evans
Fish (Marillion) .... Derek Dick
Grandmaster Flash................ Joseph Saddler
Billy Idol................................. William Broad
Chaka Khan............................. Yvette Stevens
Kid Creole .... Thomas August Darnell Browder
Kiki Dee .... Pauline Matthews
LL Cool J................................. James Todd Smith
Iggy Pop .... James Jewel Osterberg
Queen Latifah .... Dana Owens
Axl Rose.................................. William Bailey
Shabba Ranks .... Rexton Gordon
Muddy Waters .... McKinley Morganfield

ADAM ANT

Similarly sometimes artists decide to change their name from something normal, to something equally or even more normal...!

Marc Bolan .... Mark Feld
David Bowie............................ David Jones
Elkie Brooks............................ Elaine Bookbinder
Jimmy Cliff.............................. James Chambers

Artist Trivia

Elvis Costello	Declan McManus
Bobby Darin	Walton Robert Cassotto
Chris DeBurgh	Christopher John Davidson
Desmond Dekker	Desmond Dacres
John Denver	John Henry Deutschendorf
Neil Diamond	Noah Kaminsky
Bob Dylan	Robert Zimmerman
Macy Gray	Natalie Renee McIntyre
Tom Jones	Thomas Woodward
Ben E King	Benjamin Earl Nelson
Paul McCartney	James Paul McCartney
Barry Manilow	Barry Alan Pinkus
George Michael	Georgios Kyriacos Panayioutu
Billy Ocean	Leslie Sebastian Charles
Lou Reed	Louis Firbank
Edwin Starr	Steve Harrington
Joe Strummer	John Mellor
Donna Summer	Ladonna Gaines
Tina Turner	Anna Mae Bullock

Rap artists have a tendency to change their names to something more 'street'. Here are some of the best:

Big Boi (OutKast)	Antwan Patton
Busta Rhymes	Trevor Smith
Dizzee Rascal	Dylan Mills
Dr Dre	Andre Young
Easy E	Eric Wright
Eminem	Marshall Mathers
50 Cent	Curtis Jackson
The Game	Jayceon Taylor
Ice Cube	O'shea Jackson
MC Hammer	Stanley Kirk Burrell
Ice-T	Tracy Morrow
Nelly	Cornell Haynes
Notorious B.I.G.	Christopher Wallace
Ol' Dirty Bastard	Russell Jones
Snoop Doggy Dogg	Calvin Broadus
Vanilla Ice	Robert Van Winkle

BIG BOI (OUTKAST)

75

BEFORE THEY WERE FAMOUS

Professions of our pop personalities before fame struck...

NICOLAS GODIN (AIR)
Architect

JULIANNE REGAN (ALL ABOUT EVE)
Music Journalist

TASMIN ARCHER
Clerk at a magistrates court

GARY BARLOW (TAKE THAT)
Cabaret club pianist, supported artists such as Ken Dodd

CHUCK BERRY
Hairdresser/Janitor

BILLIE
Bit part in *Eastenders*, and the face of *Smash Hits*

CILLA BLACK
Hat check girl at the Cavern, Liverpool

MARC BOLAN
Extra on ITV children's show
Five O'Clock Club

**MIKEY GRAHAM &
KEITH DUFFY
(BOYZONE)**
Mechanics

GARTH BROOKS
Bouncer

BOYZONE

MARC BOLAN

IAN DURY

JAMES BROWN
Professional bantamweight boxer

JOHNNY CASH
An airman in the US Air Force

CHER
Backing singer for The Ronettes

JOE COCKER
Plumber

LEONARD COHEN
Poet

ELVIS COSTELLO
Computer programmer

JIM CROCE
University campus radio
broadcaster

SHERYL CROW
Backing singer for both Rod Stewart and Joe Cocker

RAY DAVIES (THE KINKS)
Assistant in architects office

DESMOND DEKKER
Welder

THOMAS DOLBY
Session musician for Foreigner and Def Leppard

IAN DURY
Teacher/Lecturer at Canterbury College

BOB DYLAN
Debt Collector

JOHN ENTWISTLE
Tax clerk

BRYAN FERRY
Teacher

A FLOCK OF SEAGULLS

MIKE SCORE (A FLOCK OF SEAGULLS)
Hairdresser

PETER GABRIEL
Milliner

SIR BOB GELDOF
Ex-NME journalist

GARY GLITTER
Warm up man on *Ready Steady Go*

STEVE HARLEY (COCKNEY REBEL)
Journalist

DEBBIE HARRY
Playboy Club Bunny

**MARTYN WARE & IAN CRAIG MARSH
(HUMAN LEAGUE)**
Computer operators

CHRISSIE HYNDE (THE PRETENDERS)
Selling leather handbags on London's Oxford Street

MICK JAGGER
Hospital porter

BILLY JOEL
Welter-weight boxing champion

GRACE JONES
Model (appeared on front cover of *Vogue* magazine).

Artist Trivia

HOWARD JONES
Factory worker

RICKIE LEE JONES
Waitress in Los Angeles restaurant

KRIS KRISTOFFERSON
US football star/Night janitor at Columbia Records

MARK KNOPFLER
Teacher/Journalist

LENNY KRAVITZ
Actor – appeared in commercials for Burger King

CYNDI LAUPER
Clothes store worker at *Screaming Mimi's* in New York

NEIL BARNES (LEFTFIELD)
English teacher

HUEY LEWIS (HUEY LEWIS & THE NEWS)
Yogurt factory worker

GORDON LIGHTFOOT
Jingle writer

LITTLE RICHARD
Seller of snake oil at fairs,
Dr. Hudson's Medicine Show

JENNIFER LOPEZ
Dancer/choreographer

JENNIFER LOPEZ

BRYAN MacLEAN (LOVE)
A roadie for The Byrds

DON McCLEAN
Club singer called 'The Hudson River Troubadour'

MADONNA
Waitress and part-time model (nude photos were published
in 1985 by *Playboy* & *Penthouse* magazines)

BARRY MANILOW
CBS Mailroom in Manhattan

BARRY MANILOW

KYLIE MINOGUE
Actress, first appearing in various
Australian soaps

JONI MITCHELL
Department store shop assistant

ALANIS MORISSETTE
Child actress. At the age of 10 appearing on the Nickelodeon
show *You Can't Do That On Television* alongside *Friends* star
Matt LeBlanc

NICO
Model, and bit actress

NOEL GALLAGHER (OASIS)
British Gas storeman/Guitar technician for the Inspiral Carpets
(he originally auditioned for the Inspiral Carpets as lead singer,
and failing that was offered the job as guitar technician)

BILLY OCEAN
Tailor, working on Savile Row

HAZEL O'CONNOR
English teacher/dancer/nude model

OZZY OSBOURNE

OZZY OSBOURNE
Abattoir worker

**GEOFF BARROW
(PORTISHEAD)**
Builder

ELVIS PRESLEY
Truck driver

CHRIS REA
Labourer/ice-cream salesman

**RICKY ROSS
(DEACON BLUE)**
Teacher

SADE
Model

STING
Teacher

KEVIN GODLEY/LOL CREME (10CC)
Designers for children's books

NEIL TENNANT
Editor for *Smash Hits*

SHARLEEN SPITERI (TEXAS)
Hairdresser

KIAN (WESTLIFE)
Kissogram

CHRIS REA

GUEST APPEARANCES: INSTRUMENTALISTS

*From time to time stars turn up on each others records.
Here are some classics and surprises!*

JON BON JOVI
Wrote and played the guitar on Stevie Nicks' *'Sometimes It's
A Bitch'*

DAVID BOWIE

Played the saxophone on 'All The Young Dudes' by Mott The Hoople, a track which he also wrote. Bowie has also appeared on numerous Lou Reed and Iggy Pop songs

ERIC CLAPTON

To list all of Clapton's guest appearances would be a lengthy task. Clapton has contributed guitar and vocals to a huge amount of songs, notably, 'City Blues' by Brian Wilson (from *Getting Over My Head*), 'The Calling' on Santana's *Supernatural* album, and 'We're Only In It For The Money' by Frank Zappa. He has also guested on songs by The Band, Lionel Richie, Kate Bush, The Rolling Stones and The Beatles amongst others

PHIL COLLINS

Is the drummer on 'Woman In Chains' by Tears For Fears, and has also appeared as drummer/percussionist on numerous other albums including *Grace And Danger* by John Martyn (for which Collins was also the producer), *Harbour Lights* by Bruce Hornsby, *Break Every Rule* by Tina Turner, as well as many albums by Eric Clapton, Brian Eno, Peter Gabriel and Robert Plant

KING CURTIS

Is the sax player on 'Respect' by Aretha Franklin (this song was written by Otis Redding)

JOHNNY DEPP

Plays slide guitar on 'Fade In-Out' by Oasis, and on 'That Woman's Got Me Drinking' by Shane MacGowan (he also appeared on the groups *Top Of The Pops* debut)

BOB DYLAN

Has collaborated with numerous artists over the years, from playing Hammond organ on 'Hawkmoon' by U2 (*Rattle And Hum*), harmonica on 'Boots Of Spanish Leather' for Nanci Griffith, to contributing vocals, organ, piano and guitar on a number of albums by Allen Ginsberg amongst others

ERIC CLAPTON

PETER GABRIEL
Played flute on 'Lady D'Arbanville' by Cat Stevens

NOEL GALLAGHER
Has appeared on a number of songs, he played bass on 'Shootdown' by The Prodigy (where Liam also sang vocals), acoustic guitar on 'I Walk On Gilded Splinters' by Paul Weller, and is also featured on tracks by Cornershop, The Chemical Brothers and Beck amongst others

DIZZY GILLESPIE
Was the trumpet player on 'Do I Do' by Stevie Wonder

GEORGE HARRISON
Played guitar on 'Badge' by Cream, a song he also co-wrote, as well as appearing on many other albums including *Runaway Horses* by Belinda Carlisle and *Zoom* by Electric Light Orchestra

BRUCE HORNSBY
Appeared playing piano and singing on Clannad's *Sirius* album on the songs 'Second Nature' and 'Something To Believe In'

BILLY JOEL
Is the pianist on the Shangri-La's hit 'Leader Of The Pack'

DR. JOHN
Played organ on Aretha Franklin's single 'Spanish Harlem'

ELTON JOHN
A young Elton played the piano for 'He Ain't Heavy, He's My Brother' by The Hollies. He has also contributed vocals and piano/keyboards to many other artists albums, notably, *Mary* (Mary J. Blige), *Cloud Nine* (George Harrison), *Under The Red Sky* (Bob Dylan), *Blaze Of Glory* (Jon Bon Jovi) and *Together* (Lulu)

LENNY KRAVITZ
Is the guitarist on David Bowie's 'Buddah Of Suburbia', 'Maybe' by N.E.R.D., 'PMS' by Mary J. Blige, and multi-instrumentalist on

'Time Of Our Life' by Lionel Richie. Kravitz also performs with Mick Jagger on 'God Gave Me Everything' as well has having collaborated with Madonna, Vanessa Paradis, Baha Men and Busta Rhymes

TOMMY LEE (MÖTLEY CRÜE)

Rather strangely, is the drummer on 'I Get No Sleep' by smoothie Richard Marx

PAUL McCARTNEY

Is the drummer on 'Back On The U.S.S.R.' and 'The Ballad Of John And Yoko and the kazoo player on 'You're Sixteen' by Ringo Starr. He also played bass on Steve Miller's 'My Dark Hour' (under the pseudonym Mark Ramon) to name but a few

KEITH MOON

Was the drummer on 'Ole Man River' by the Jeff Beck Group and also played percussion on *Pussy Cats* by Harry Nilsson and John Lennon

JIMMY PAGE

Is the guitarist on 'I Can't Explain' by The Who, and 'Sunshine Superman' by Donovan. Page is also lead guitarist on Joe Cocker's version of 'With A Little Help From My Friends'. Page has made, and is still making appearances on numerous albums, including *Dirty Work* (The Rolling Stones), *Blow Up* (The Primitives), and more recently on the single 'Come With Me' by P Diddy

'SLASH' FROM GUNS N' ROSES

Played guitar on two tracks from *Mama Said* by Lenny Kravitz

JIMMY PAGE

PHIL SPECTOR

Is the pianist on 'Out Of Our Heads' by The Rolling Stones, he also provided piano/keyboards on Leonard Cohen's *Death Of A Ladies Man* and on 'Love' with John Lennon and The Plastic Ono Band

STEPHEN STILLS

Played lead guitar on 'Ain't No Sunshine' by Bill Withers

ROGER TAYLOR (QUEEN)

Is the drummer on 'She's Got Claws' by Gary Numan

EDDIE VAN HALEN

Is the guitarist on Michael Jackson's 'Beat It'

PAUL WELLER

Played the organ on 'The Riverboat Song' by Ocean Colour Scene, sang backing vocals and played guitar on 'Champagne Supernova' and lead guitar and harmonica on 'The Swamp Song', both by Oasis. Weller has also contributed to songs by Primal Scream, The Beautiful South, Peter Gabriel and Death In Vegas

Artist Trivia

PAUL WELLER

OLETA ADAMS
Is the vocalist on 'Woman In Chains' by Tears For Fears

CAPTAIN BEEFHEART
Is the lead vocalist on Frank Zappa's 'Hot Rats'

ANDY BELL (ERASURE)
Sings backing vocals on Ant & Dec's 'Shout'

KATE BUSH
Has contributed vocals to songs by Peter Gabriel, Prince, Big Country, Go West, Midge Ure and Roy Harper

CHAKA KHAN
Sings backing vocals on Steve Winwood's 'Higher Love'

PHIL COLLINS
Sings backing vocals on 'Bad Love' by Eric Clapton

BOB DYLAN
Contributed backing vocals to 'Don't Go Home With Your Hard-On' by Leonard Cohen, 'Love Rescue Me' by U2, 'All Things Must Pass' by George Harrison, and many other tracks

MARIANNE FAITHFULL
Sings backing vocals on Metallica's *The Memory Remains*, Ryan Adams' *Love Is Hell* album and also appeared in the chorus of 'All You Need Is Love' by The Beatles

MARIANNE FAITHFULL

ELIZABETH FRASER (COCTEAU TWINS)

Fraser's ethereal vocals have featured on many tracks, the stand out songs being 'Teardrop' (Massive Attack), 'This Love' (Craig Armstrong) and on *Lifeforms* with the Future Sound Of London

ALISON GOLDFRAPP

Is the female vocalist on 'Pumpkin' and 'Sad But True' by Tricky, and 'Are We Here' by Orbital

NEIL HANNON AND NEIL TENNANT

Are vocalists on the Robbie Williams single 'No Regrets'

KIRSTY MacCOLL

Sang backing vocals on Morrissey's 'Interesting Drug', as well as featuring on songs by David Byrne, The Wonder Stuff, The Pogues, and Simple Minds, amongst others

JOHN LENNON AND PAUL McCARTNEY

Sings backing vocals on 'We Love You/Dandelion' by The Rolling Stones

PAUL McCARTNEY

Sings backing vocals on Donovan's 'Mellow Yellow'

MARIA McKEE

Sang backing vocals on Counting Crows debut album *August And Everything After*

RICHARD MARX

Is a featured backing singer on 'White Heat' from Madonna's *True Blue* album

JONI MITCHELL

Sings backing vocals with James Taylor on 'Will You Love Me Tomorrow' from Carole King's *Tapestry*. They are credited as "The Mitchell/Taylor Boy-and-Girl Choir"

JONI MITCHELL

JIMMY NAIL
Sings backing vocals on
'This Cowboy Song' by Sting

SINEAD O'CONNOR
Sang on the 1989 The The song
'Kingdom Of Rain'

LINDA RONSTADT AND
JAMES TAYLOR
Are the backing vocalists on
Neil Young's 'Heart Of Gold'

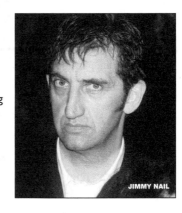
JIMMY NAIL

PATTI SMITH
Sings backing vocals on 'E-Bow The Letter' by R.E.M.

PATTI SMITH

STING
Sang the line "I want my MTV" on Dire Straits' 'Money For Nothing'. Sting has guested on numerous other albums, notably *No Jacket Required* (Phil Collins), *Wildest Dreams* (Tina Turner) and *You're Under Arrest* (Frank Zappa)

THE TEMPTATIONS
Sang backing vocals for Bruce Willis on his version of 'Under The Boardwalk'

LUTHER VANDROSS
Sang backing vocals on Stevie Wonder's 'Part Time Lover'

JACK WHITE
Contributed backing vocals to the 2002 re-recording of 'Danger! High Voltage' by Electric 6

STING

BRIAN WILSON
Sings backing vocals on 'California' by Belinda Carlisle

TRIBUTED TO...

Often artists tribute or write a song to a special person, or a particular influence. Here are a selection of tributes:

'AMERICAN PIE'
By Don McLean was dedicated to Buddy Holly

'AND I LOVE HER'
Was written by Paul McCartney about his then-girlfriend
Jane Asher

'ANGEL OF HARLEM'
By U2 is a tribute to Billie Holiday

'ANGIE'
By The Rolling Stones, was written by Mick Jagger and
Keith Richards about Angela, David Bowie's first wife

'BABY YOU'RE A RICH MAN'
Was written by Lennon & McCartney about their manager
Brian Epstein

'CARRIE ANNE'
This Hollies song was written about Marianne Faithfull

'CHELSEA HOTEL #2'
Leonard Cohen's tribute to Janis Joplin who overdosed in 1970

'FREE BIRD'
By Lynryd Skynyrd is a tribute to Duane Allman from the
Allman Brothers

'HEY JUDE'
Was written about John Lennon's son, Julian

'HOW DO YOU SLEEP'
Written by John Lennon, it was about Paul McCartney

'I'LL KEEP IT WITH MINE'
Bob Dylan wrote this for Nico

'JEAN GENIE'
Is Bowie's tribute to Iggy Pop

'JULIA'
Was a tribute to John Lennon's mother

DAVID BOWIE

'JUST THE WAY YOU ARE'
Was written by Billy Joel as a birthday present
for his wife Elizabeth

'LAYLA'
Was written about Eric Clapton's love for George Harrison's
then-wife Patty Boyd Harrison. Eric and Patti later married

'MARTHA MY DEAR'
Was written by Paul McCartney about Martha,
his English sheepdog

'MASTER BLASTER'
Was Stevie Wonder's tribute to Bob Marley

'MOONLIGHT SHADOW'
Mike Oldfield's tribute to John Lennon

'OH! CAROL'
Neil Sedaka wrote this song in 1959, and dedicated it to
his high-school girlfriend Carol Klein, later to be known as
Carole King

'PEGGY SUE'
The real life 'Peggy Sue' that Buddy Holly sang about was Peggy
Sue Gerron, the girlfriend of his drummer, Jerry Allison. The song
was initially titled 'Cindy Lou', but Allison convinced Buddy to
change the title just before the recording session. Allison and
Gerron were later married

'PHILADELPHIA FREEDOM'
Is Elton John's tribute to tennis star Billie Jean King

'SHINE ON YOU CRAZY DIAMOND'
By Pink Floyd was inspired by their ex-frontman, Syd Barrett

'SISTER'
Bros wrote 'Sister' a number 10 hit in 1989, dedicated to their
sister who had been killed in a car crash

'SOLID AIR'
John Martyn wrote this classic, for good friend Nick Drake

'STUCK IN A MOMENT YOU CAN'T GET OUT OF'
Bono wrote this song for his friend Michael Hutchence who died under mysterious circumstances

SUITE FOR SUSAN MOORE AND DAMIEN (ALBUM)
Was written by Tim Hardin for his wife and son

MICHAEL HUTCHENCE

'TEARS IN HEAVEN'
Eric Clapton wrote this song for his dead son Connor

'VINCENT'
By Don McLean was written about Vincent Van Gogh

'WALKING ON THIN ICE'
Was a tribute to John Lennon by Yoko Ono

'WESTSIDE'
By TQ is dedicated to Tupac Shakur and Easy-E (from N.W.A.)

'WHEN I'M SIXTY-FOUR'
Was written about Paul McCartney's father, James

'YEAR OF THE CAT'
By Al Stewart is written about the late comedian Tony Hancock

Over the years, there has been a huge amount of 'borrowing' of other peoples material, especially before sampling became the norm. Here's a list of some of the worst acts of plagiarism. For official use of samples, see the sampling list on page 124

'MY SWEET LORD'

On February 10th, 1971, Bright Tunes Music Corp. filed a suit against George Harrison for plagiarism owing to the similarities between 'He's So Fine' by The Chiffons and Harrison's own 'My Sweet Lord'. Although Harrison always claimed the resemblance was unintentional, the presiding judge said it was "Perfectly obvious...the two songs are virtually identical" and awarded damages. Ironically in 1975 The Chiffons recorded their own version of 'My Sweet Lord'

RITCHIE VALENS

'LA BAMBA'

The 1958 million seller for Ritchie Valens is a traditional song that can be traced back as far as the 14th century. The tune was picked up by the people of Mexico after they heard homesick African slaves singing about their village of Mamamba in the 1800s

'TELSTAR'

The French film composer Jean Ledrut sued Joe Meek claiming that 'Telstar' plagiarised the soundtrack to his film *The Battle Of Austerlitz*

'I CAN'T EXPLAIN'

The Who's 'I Can't Explain' has been greatly likened to The Kinks song 'You Really Got Me'. Entwistle even claimed that its creation was the result of Townshend "misremembering" the Ray Davies classic

Artist Trivia

JOHNNY CASH

'FOLSOM PRISON BLUES'

Gordon Jenkins successfully sued Johnny Cash due to the likeness between Jenkins' 'Crescent City Blues' and Cash's 'Folsom Prison Blues'. Recent writer credits of the song now include both Jenkins and Cash

'HARVEST FOR THE WORLD'

The Isley Brothers won a $5 million law suit in 2001 by successfully proving that Michael Bolton's 'Love Is A Wonderful Thing' plagiarised their own 'Harvest For The World'

'GOOD TIMES'

The Sugar Hill Gang gave virtually all of the profits generated by their hit single 'Rappers Delight' to Bernard Edwards and Nile Rogers of Chic, who rightly claimed that the song used rhythms from their hit single 'Good Times'

'GHOSTBUSTERS'

Ray Parker Jnr. paid an out of court settlement to Huey Lewis & The News for plagiarising their song 'I Want A New Drug (Called Love)' on his song 'Ghostbusters'

'GUNS OF BRIXTON'

Beats International's number 1 hit 'Dub Be Good To Me' stole the bassline from 'Guns Of Brixton' by The Clash, and also from the S.O.S. Band's 'Just Be Good To Me'

Videos today are seen by some to be as important as the music, so for very lavish affairs, celebrities are brought in to perform cameo roles

PAMELA ANDERSON
'Miserable' (Lit)

KIM BASINGER
'Mary Jane's Last Dance' (Tom Petty)

JOAN COLLINS
'Spitting In The Wind' (Badly Drawn Boy)

SOFIA COPPOLA
'Electrobank' (The Chemical Brothers)

COURTNEY COX
'Dancing In The Dark' (Bruce Springsteen)/
'A Long December' (Counting Crows)

HELENA CHRISTENSEN
'Wicked Game'
(Chris Isaak)

JOHNNY DEPP
'Into The Great Wide Open'
(Tom Petty)

ROBERT DOWNEY JUNIOR
'I Want Love' (Elton John)

FRENCH & SAUNDERS
'Love Letters' (Alison Moyet)

JOHNNY DEPP

PAMELA ANDERSON

SARAH MICHELLE GELLAR
'Sour Girl' (Stone Temple Pilots)

ANGELINA JOLIE
'Has Anybody Seen My Baby' (The Rolling Stones)/
'Did My Time' (Korn)

MATT LEBLANC
'Night Moves' (Bob Seger)

KATE MOSS
'I Just Don't Know What To Do With Myself' (The White Stripes)

ANGELINA JOLIE

GWYNETH PALTROW
'I Wanna Come Over' (Melissa Etheridge)

KEANU REEVES
'Rush Rush' (Paula Abdul)

DONALD SUTHERLAND
'Cloudbusting' (Kate Bush)

JUSTIN TIMBERLAKE
'This Train Don't Stop Here Any More' (Elton John)

LIV TYLER
'Crazy' (Aerosmith)

CHRISTOPHER WALKEN
'Weapon Of Choice' (Fatboy Slim)/'Bad Girl' (Madonna)

ELIJAH WOOD
'Ridiculous Thoughts' (The Cranberries)/
'Forever Your Girl' (Paula Abdul)

THE DANGEROUS CROSS-OVER INTO FILM

Most of the time it should never be done... here's a list of those who have strayed into the movies

BJÖRK
Dancer In The Dark, The Juniper Tree, Pret A Porter

JON BON JOVI
Has starred in 18 films including, *Young Guns II, Moonlight and Valentino, The Leading Man, Vampires: Los Muertos*

DAVID BOWIE
The Man Who Fell To Earth, Just A Gigolo, The Hunger, Merry Christmas Mr Lawrence, Into The Night, Labyrinth, Absolute Beginners, The Last Temptation Of Christ, The Linguini Incident, Basquait

BOBBY BROWN
Ghostbusters II

IAN BROWN (STONE ROSES)
Harry Potter & The Prisoner Of Askaban

KATE BUSH
The Red Shoes

NICK CAVE
Ghosts... Of The Civil Dead, Stadt, Die, Rhinoceros Hunting In Budapest, Johnny Suede

CHER
Has starred in 16 films including, *Mask, Suspect, Moonstruck, Silkwood, Mermaids, The Witches Of Eastwick, Tea With Mussolini*

KATE BUSH

BOB DYLAN
Has starred in nine films including, *Hearts Of Fire,
Renaldo & Clara, Pat Garrett & Billy The Kid*

EMINEM
Eight Mile

'FLEA' (RED HOT CHILI PEPPERS)
Has had bit parts and provided character voices for numerous
films, including *My Own Private Idaho, The Big Lebowski,* and *Psycho*
(the 1998 remake)

DEBBIE HARRY

ARETHA FRANKLIN
The Blues Brothers

GOLDIE
James Bond: The World Is Not Enough

DEBBIE HARRY
*Union City, Roadie, Videodrome,
Hairspray*

MICHAEL HUTCHENCE
Dogs In Space and *Frankenstein
Unbound*

CHRIS ISAAK
The Silence Of The Lambs, Married To The Mob

MICK JAGGER
Has starred in 11 films including, *Performance, Ned Kelly,
Enigma, Mayor Of The Sunset Strip*

GRACE JONES
Has starred in 15 films including, *Conan The Destroyer* and
James Bond: A View To A Kill

BEYONCE KNOWLES
Austin Powers: Goldmember

JENNIFER LOPEZ
Has appeared in 26 films, including *The Wedding Planner*,
Maid In Manhattan and *Gigli*

COURTNEY LOVE
Has appeared in 12 films including, *The People vs. Larry Flynt*,
and *Sid & Nancy*

MADONNA
Has appeared in 22 films, notably, *Desperately Seeking Susan*, *Evita*,
Body Of Evidence, and *Die Another Day*

DOLLY PARTON
Straight Talk, *Steel Magnolias*, *Rhinestone*, *The Best Little Whorehouse
In Texas*, *Nine To Five*

ELVIS PRESLEY
Has starred in 31 films including: *Love Me Tender*, *G I Blues*, *Blue
Hawaii* and *Frankie & Johnny*

BRITNEY SPEARS
Crossroads

BRITNEY SPEARS

Artist Trivia

TOYAH

MEAT LOAF
Has starred in 30 films including: *Fight Club*, *The Rocky Horror Picture Show*, *Wayne's World*

JOE STRUMMER
Lost In Space and *Straight To Hell*

TOYAH
Jubilee, *The Corn Is Green*, *Quadrophenia*, *The Tempest*

TINA TURNER
Has featured in four films, *The Goddess*, *Last Action Hero*, *Mad Max Beyond Thunderdome* and *Tommy*

STEVE VAI
Crossroads

DONNIE WAHLBERG
(NEW KIDS ON THE BLOCK)
Has appeared in 18 films including *The Sixth Sense*.

MARK WAHLBERG
Has starred in 20 films, notably *The Basketball Diaries*, *Boogie Nights*, *The Perfect Storm*, *Planet Of The Apes* and *I Heart Huckabees*

Quite often pop stars are rewarded by the State for their contribution to music and the arts. Here's a list of some of the recipients:

SIR CLIFF RICHARD

Artist Trivia

KNIGHTHOODs
Paul McCartney
Elton John
Mick Jagger
Cliff Richard
Bob Geldof
George Martin
Shirley Bassey
Peter Blake (The Beatles
Sgt. Pepper artwork)

MBEs
Noddy Holder
John Lennon (sent his back
in 1969 in protest of the
Vietnam War)
Paul McCartney
Ringo Starr
George Harrison
Gerry Marsden (Gerry & The Pacemakers)

OBEs
Sade
Van Morrison
Errol Brown
Lulu
Mark Knopfler
Jools Holland
Roger Daltrey

JOOLS HOLLAND

CBEs
The Bee Gees
Sting

Dave Gilmour (Pink Floyd)
Eric Clapton
Ray Davies (The Kinks)

THE FOLLOWING STARS BOTH TURNED DOWN THE CBE:
George Melly
David Bowie

Chapter 6
Song Lists

JANE BIRKIN &
SERGE GAINSBOURG

RECORDS BANNED!

A selection of songs they didn't want you to hear…

THE ANTI-NOWHERE LEAGUE 'SO WHAT?' (1981)

This song was so lyrically offensive, it was not only banned by radio stations and high street stores, but also seized by the Obscene Publications Squad. The lyrics are even too obscene to quote in this book!

THE BEATLES 'A DAY IN THE LIFE'/ 'LUCY IN THE SKY WITH DIAMONDS' (1967)

The BBC claimed these songs contained specific references to drugs

THE BEATLES 'COME TOGETHER' (1969)

Due to the reference to *Coca-Cola*, the song was banned for advertising reasons

MIKE BERRY 'TRIBUTE TO BUDDY HOLLY' (1961)

This was denied airplay as it apparently displayed a "morbid concern" for the dead singer

JANE BIRKIN & SERGE GAINSBOURG 'JE T'AIME… MOI NON PLUS' (1969)

Banned because of its licentious lyrical content and heavy breathing

THE BLOW MONKEYS 'THE DAY AFTER YOU' (1987)

This record was banned for supposedly being anti Margaret Thatcher

CROSBY, STILLS, NASH & YOUNG 'OHIO' (1970)

Following shootings at an Ohio state university, this record was banned as more violence was feared

Song Lists

CROWDED HOUSE
'SIX MONTHS IN A LEAKY BOAT'
Banned by BBC in 1982 due to the Falklands conflict

BOBBY DARIN 'MACK THE KNIFE' (1959)
Banned due to juvenile stabbings in New York City

THE DEAD KENNEDY'S
'TOO DRUNK TO F**K' (1981)
Despite this song being banned for its obvious lyrical content, it was the first song to chart in the UK with the 'f' word in the title

BOBBY DARIN

D MOB 'WE CALL IT ACIEEED' (1988)
Banned for promoting the use of drugs in the 80s club culture

FRANKIE GOES TO HOLLYWOOD
'RELAX' (1983)
BBC Radio 1 DJ Mike Read cited a ban because of the sexual references and much use of the word "come"

HAWKWIND 'URBAN GUERILLA' (1973)
Banned because of the UK terrorist attacks which were rife at that time

BILLIE HOLIDAY 'LOVE FOR SALE' (1956)
Because the song was about prostitution

THE KINGSMEN 'LOUIE, LOUIE' (1964)
Because of the indecipherable lyrics, which were thought to contain rude words, with a bad subliminal message

THE KINKS 'LOLA' (1970)
Banned because of the advertising reference to *Coca-Cola*. Later this was changed to cherry cola

JOHN LENNON 'WOMAN IS THE NIGGER OF THE WORLD' (1972)
Due to its obviously controversial title and content

Song Lists

JOHN LENNON & YOKO ONO
TWO VIRGINS **ALBUM (1969)**
The cover showed Lennon & Ono naked, resulting in 30,000 copies seized by American police

LORETTA LYNN 'BIRTH CONTROL' (1975)
Due to the references to, strangely, birth control

PAUL McCARTNEY
'GIVE IRELAND BACK TO THE IRISH' (1972)
The BBC banned the song because it dared to speak out about the Britain/Ireland conflict

BARRY McGUIRE 'EVE OF DESTRUCTION' (1965)
This release wasn't supported due to its Armageddon theme

GEORGE MICHAEL 'I WANT YOUR SEX' (1987)
Banned by many American radio stations as well as the BBC because of its explicit sexual content

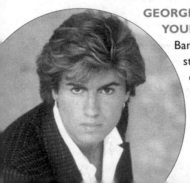

GEORGE MICHAEL

THE MONKEES 'RANDY SCOUSE GIT'
A song based on the Alf Garnett character from *Til Death Do Us Part* was banned by the BBC because of its title. It was renamed 'Alternative Title' and reached number 2 in 1967

VAN MORRISON 'BROWN EYED GIRL' (1967)
Originally the song mentioned premarital sex and teenage pregnancy. (Morrison however changed the lyrics and recorded an alternative version which became his first solo US hit)

NAPOLEON XIV 'THEY'RE COMING TO TAKE ME AWAY, HA-HAAA!' (1966)
Was a number 3 hit in America, but banned by many radio stations because it was thought that it made fun of the insane

OLIVIA NEWTON JOHN 'PHYSICAL' (1981)
Banned in some American states because of the sexual innuendoes

RAY PETERSON 'TELL LAURA I LOVE HER' (1960)
Because of the death theme to the song. Ricky Valance did a cover version of it, which went to number 1 in the British charts

BOBBY "BORIS" PICKETT 'MONSTER MASH' (1962)
For its vaguely satanic overtones

THE POLICE 'I CAN'T STAND LOSING YOU' (1978)
The song is a suicide letter, and was considered too much for teenagers to hear

THE POLICE 'INVISIBLE SUN' (1981)
Because of political references to Northern Ireland

THE PRODIGY 'SMACK MY BITCH UP' (1997)
This single had been out for almost six months before the record was banned, selling over 150,000 copies without one customer complaint

CLIFF RICHARD 'HONKY TONK ANGELS' (1973)

Banned by Cliff Richard himself as he apparently had no idea he was singing about prostitution!

THE ROLLING STONES
'I CAN'T GET NO SATISFACTION' (1965)

Because of the sexually suggestive lyrics

THE ROLLING STONES
'LET'S SPEND THE NIGHT TOGETHER' (1967)

It was thought this record condoned sexual promiscuity

THE ROLLING STONES 'STAR STAR' (1973)

Because the lyrics contain the word star-f**ker, which is repeated many times in the chorus

THE ROLLING STONES
'STREET FIGHTING MAN' (1968)

It was thought that the song might incite violence during the National Democratic Convention which was happening at that time. Oddly, despite the ban riots still occurred

MAX ROMEO 'WET DREAM' (1969)

Banned by the BBC for obvious reasons…

RESZO SERESS 'GLOOMY SUNDAY' (1932)

Written by Hungarian songwriter Seress, this song seemed to be the cause of a number of suicides, initially in Hungary, but as the song was translated and performed by artists such as Billie Holiday, more suicides occurred in Europe and America. Eventually the BBC and other radio stations banned it

SEX PISTOLS 'GOD SAVE THE QUEEN' (1977)

This was released to coincide with the Queen's Silver Jubilee celebrations, and banned from British airplay because of its "treasonous sentiments"

THE SEX PISTOLS

This song is still the most heavily censored record in British popular music history despite reaching number 2 in the UK charts

THE SHAMEN 'EBENEEZER GOODE' (1993)
Banned by the BBC for its alleged pro-ecstasy lyrics. Despite the ban, the single still topped the British charts

PAUL SIMON 'ME AND JULIO DOWN BY THE SCHOOLYARD' (1972)
The song contained a reference to *Newsweek* magazine, and was therefore deemed as advertising

DONNA SUMMER 'LOVE TO LOVE YOU' (1976)
The groans and heavy breathing in the record were seen as being inappropriate

SUPER FURRY ANIMALS 'THE MAN DON'T GIVE A F**K' (1996)
Banned due to 53 uses of the F-word

TOM ROBINSON BAND 'GLAD TO BE GAY' (1978)
This gay rights anthem was too much for the BBC!

RICKY VALANCE 'TELL LAURA I LOVE HER' (1960)
The song is about a man who dies in a stock car race. It was banned by the BBC because of the morbid theme

THE WHO 'PICTURES OF LILY' (1965)
Banned because of the reference to masturbation in the song

WINGS 'HI HI HI' (1973)
Banned due to its inappropriate and sexual lyrics: "I want to lie on the bed, get you ready for my polygon. I'm gonna do it to you, gonna do it, sweet banana, you've never been done. Yes, I go like a rabbit, gonna grab it, gonna do it 'til the night is done"

LINK WRAY - INSTRUMENTAL 'RUMBLE' (1959)
Because it was thought that the title promoted teen violence

CHRISTMAS NUMBER Is

The Big Daddy of number 1s

1952 'Here In My Heart' Al Martino

1953 'Answer Me' Frankie Laine/
David Whitfield

1954 'Let's Have Another Party'
Winifred Atwell

1955 'Christmas Alphabet' Dickie Valentine

AL MARTINO

1956 'Just Walking In The Rain' Johnnie Ray

1957 'Mary's Boy Child' Harry Belafonte

1958 'It's Only Make Believe' Conway Twitty

1959 'What Do You Want To Make Those Eyes At Me For?'
Emile Ford & The Checkmates

1960 'I Love You' Cliff Richard & The Shadows

1961 'Moon River' Danny Williams with
Geoff Love & His Orchestra

1962 'Return To Sender' Elvis Presley & The Jordanires

1963 'I Want To Hold Your Hand' The Beatles

1964 'I Feel Fine' The Beatles

1965 'Day Tripper/We Can Work It Out' The Beatles

1966 'Green Green Grass Of Home' Tom Jones

1967 'Hello Goodbye' The Beatles

1968 'Lily The Pink' Scaffold

1969 'Two Little Boys' Rolf Harris

1970 'I Hear You Knocking' Dave Edmunds Rockpile

1971 'Ernie (The Fastest Milkman In The West)' Benny Hill

Song Lists

1972 'Long Haired Lover From Liverpool'
Little Jimmy Osmond

1973 'Merry Xmas Everybody' Slade

1974 'Lonely This Christmas' Mud

1975 'Bohemian Rhapsody' Queen

1976 'When A Child Is Born (Soleado)' Johnny Mathis

1977 'Mull Of Kintyre/Girls' School' Wings

1978 'Mary's Boy Child/Oh My Lord' Boney M

1979 'Another Brick In The Wall Part II' Pink Floyd

1980 'There's No One Quite Like Grandma' St.Winifred's
School Choir

1981 'Don't You Want Me' The Human League

1982 'Save Your Love' Renee & Renato

1983 'Only You' The Flying Pickets

BAND AID

1984 'Do They Know It's Christmas?' Band Aid

1985 'Merry Christmas Everyone' Shakin' Stevens

1986 'Reet Petite (The Sweetest Girl In Town)' Jackie Wilson

1987 'Always On My Mind' The Pet Shop Boys

1988 'Mistletoe And Wine' Cliff Richard

1989 'Do They Know It's Christmas?' Band Aid II

1990 'Saviour's Day' Cliff Richard

1991 'Bohemian Rhapsody/These Are The Days
Of Our Lives' Queen

1992 'I Will Always Love You' Whitney Houston

1993 'Mr Blobby' Mr Blobby

1994 'Stay Another Day' East 17

1995 'Earth Song' Michael Jackson

1996 '2 Become 1' Spice Girls

1997 'Too Much' Spice Girls

1998 'Goodbye' Spice Girls

1999 'I Have A Dream/Seasons In The Sun' Westlife

2000 'Can We Fix It?' Bob The Builder

2001 'Something Stupid' Robbie Williams & Nicole Kidman

2002 'Sound Of The Underground' Girls Aloud

2003 'Mad World' Michael Andrews feat. Gary Jules

2004 'Do They Know It's Christmas?' Band Aid 20

NUMBER 1 COVER VERSIONS

*All the songs listed have reached number 1, but have been
previously recorded by other artists...*

SONG	COVERED BY	ORIGINAL	NUMBER 1 IN...
Always On My Mind	Pet Shop Boys	Elvis Presley	1987
American Pie	Madonna	Don McLean	2000
D.I.V.O.R.C.E.	Billy Connolly	Tammy Wynette	1975

SONG	COVERED BY	ORIGINAL	NUMBER I IN...
Dizzy	Vic Reeves & The Wonderstuff	Tommy Roe	1991
Don't Leave Me This Way	The Communards	Harold Melvin & The Bluenotes	1986
Eternal Flame	Atomic Kitten	The Bangles	2001
Evergreen	Will Young	Westlife	2002
Heaven	D J Sammy	Bryan Adams	2003
How Deep Is Your Love	Take That	The Bee Gees	1996
I Have A Dream	Westlife	ABBA	1999
I Heard It Through The Grapevine	Marvin Gaye	Smokey Robinson & The Miracles	1969
I Think We're Alone Now	Tiffany	Tommy James & The Shondells	1988
I Will Always Love You	Whitney Houston	Dolly Parton	1992
I'm A Believer	The Monkees	Neil Diamond	1967
It's Raining Men	Geri Halliwell	The Weather Girls	2001
Jealous Guy	Roxy Music	John Lennon	1981
Killing Me Softly (With His Song)	Fugees	Roberta Flack	1996
Kiss Kiss	Holly Valance	Hakim	2002
Lady Marmalade	Christina Aguilera/ L'il Kim/Pink/Mya	Patti Labelle	2001
The Lion Sleeps Tonight	Tight Fit	The Tokens	1982
The Long & Winding Road	Will Young & Gareth Gates	The Beatles	2002
Lucille	Kenny Rogers	Johnny Darrell	1977
Mad World	Michael Andrews feat. Gary Jules	Tears For Fears	2003
Mambo No. 5*	Lou Bega	Prez Prado	1999
Mandy	Westlife	Barry Manilow	2003
Mighty Quinn	Manfred Mann	Bob Dylan	1968
Mr Tambourine Man	The Byrds	Bob Dylan	1965
Perfect Day	Various Artists	Lou Reed	1998
Red Red Wine	UB40	Neil Diamond	1983
Relight My Fire	Take That feat. Lulu	Don Hartman	1993
Sealed With A Kiss	Jason Donovan	Bryan Hyland	1989

119

SONG	COVERED BY	ORIGINAL	NUMBER I IN...
She's The One	Robbie Williams	World Party	1999
The Shoop Shoop Song (It's In His Kiss)	Cher	Betty Everett	1991
Somethin' Stupid	Robbie Williams & Nicole Kidman	Nancy Sinatra & Frank Sinatra	2001
Spirit In The Sky	Gareth Gates	Doctor & The Medics	2002
Temptation	The Everly Brothers	Bing Crosby	1961
This Ole House	Shakin' Stevens	Stuart Hamblen	1981
The Tide Is High (Get The Feeling)	Atomic Kitten	Blondie	2002
Tragedy	Steps	The Bee Gees	1999
Unchained Melody**	Robson & Jerome	Al Hibbler	1995
Under The Bridge	All Saints	Red Hot Chili Peppers	1998
Uptown Girl	Westlife	Billy Joel	2001
When The Going Gets Tough	Boyzone	Billy Ocean	1999
With A Little Help From My Friends***	Joe Cocker	The Beatles	1968
Without You	Mariah Carey	Badfinger	1994
Woodstock	Matthews Southern Comfort	Joni Mitchell	1970
Words	Boyzone	The Bee Gees	1996

*Also a number I for Bob The Builder in 2001

**Also a number I for Gareth Gates in 2002

***Also a number I for Wet Wet Wet in 1988

TOP 10 ONE HIT WONDERS

All these acts hit the top spot, but were never to reach the dizzy heights of the top 20 again...

Flat Beat	Mr Oizo	1999
Grandad	Clive Dunn	1970
Groovejet	Spiller	2000
Je T'aime... Moi Non Plus	Jane Birkin & Serge Gainsbourg	1969

Move Closer	Phyllis Nelson	1985
One Day At A Time	Lana Martell	1979
Pump Up The Volume	M/A/R/R/S	1987
Ring My Bell	Anita Ward	1979
Tell Laura I Love Her	Ricky Valance	1960
You See The Trouble With Me	Black Legend	2000

TOP 10 SONGS WITH SILLY NAMES

The following hilarious songs all hit the number 1 spot:

Blue (Da Ba De)	Eiffel 65	1999
Boom, Boom, Boom, Boom!	The Vengaboys	1999
Chirpy Chirpy Cheep Cheep	Middle Of The Road	1971
Deeply Dippy	Right Said Fred	1992
Do Wah Diddy Diddy	Manfred Mann	1964
Itsy Bitsy Teeny Weeny Yellow Polka Dot Bikini*	Bombalurina	1990
Mmmbop	Hanson	1997
My Ding-a-ling	Chuck Berry	1972
Ob-La-Di Ob-La-Da	Marmalade	1969
The Shoop Shoop Song	Cher	1991

* Also a number 8 hit for Brian Hyland in 1960

TOP 15 SONGS ABOUT ANIMALS

The following all reached number 1:

Albatross	Fleetwood Mac	1968
Beetlebum	Blur	1997
Butterfly	Andy Williams	1957
The Chicken Song	Spitting Image	1986
Eye Of The Tiger	Survivor	1982

The Fly..U2.....................................1991
(How Much Is) That Doggie...........Lita Roza.........................1953
In The Window

The Lion Sleeps Tonight..................Tight Fit............................1982
Little Red Rooster ....The Rolling Stones........1964
Puppy Love.......................................Donny Osmond............1972
Rat Trap ....The Boomtown Rats.....1978
Running Bear.....................................Johnny Preston 1960
Three Lions......................................The Lightning Seeds......1996
Tiger Feet..Mud....................................1974
Turtle Power ....Partners In Kryme 1990

JAMES BOND THEME SONGS

*The theme tunes to the James Bond films have a reputation
that exceeds any other film music. The title song tradition started
with the second film, 'From Russia With Love', although it is
Shirley Bassey's 'Goldfinger' that has proved to be the most
memorable theme. Bassey has sung two other Bond themes, and
remains to be the only singer to record more than one song.*

SEAN CONNERY

ROGER MOORE

PIERCE BROSNAN

'Live And Let Die' *and* 'The Spy Who Loved Me' *are unique among Bond themes, in that they are songs in their own right first, film themes second.* 'Live And Let Die' *has been covered by Guns N' Roses and Geri Halliwell, and was the first Bond song to make the top 10.*

SONG	FILM	ARTIST	DATE	CHART
'The James Bond Theme'	*Dr No*	John Barry	1962	11
'From Russia With Love'	*From Russia With Love*	Matt Monro	1963	20
'Goldfinger'	*Goldfinger*	Shirley Bassey	1964	21
'Thunderball'	*Thunderball*	Tom Jones	1966	35
'You Only Live Twice'	*You Only Live Twice*	Nancy Sinatra	1967	11
'We Have All The Time In The World'	*On Her Majesty's Secret Service*	Louis Armstrong	1969	-
'Diamonds Are Forever'	*Diamonds Are Forever*	Shirley Bassey	1972	38
'Live And Let Die'	*Live And Let Die*	Paul McCartney & Wings	1973	9
'The Man With The Golden Gun'	*The Man With The Golden Gun*	Lulu	1974	-
'Nobody Does It Better'	*The Spy Who Loved Me*	Carly Simon	1977	7
'Moonraker'	*Moonraker*	Shirley Bassey	1979	-
'For Your Eyes Only'	*For Your Eyes Only*	Sheena Easton	1981	8
'All Time High'	*Octopussy*	Rita Coolidge	1983	75
'Never Say Never Again'	*Never Say Never Again*	Lani Hall	1983	-
'A View To A Kill'	*A View To A Kill*	Duran Duran	1985	2
'The Living Daylights'	*The Living Daylights*	A-Ha	1987	5
'Licence To Kill'	*Licence To Kill*	Gladys Knight	1989	6
'Goldeneye'*	*Goldeneye*	Tina Turner	1995	10
'Tomorrow Never Dies'	*Tomorrow Never Dies*	Sheryl Crow	1997	12
'The World Is Not Enough'	*The World Is Not Enough*	Garbage	1999	11
'Die Another Day'	*Die Another Day*	Madonna	2002	3

* POP FACT – 'Goldeneye' was written by U2!

SAMPLED!

The art of sampling other people's music has produced some of the most ingenious moments in pop history. Here are some of the highlights:

Original Song	Originally By	Sampled By	On
Are Friends Electric?	Tubeway Army	Sugababes	Freak Like Me
Being Boiled	Human League	Richard X	Being Nobody*
Blue On Blue	Gals & Pals	Röyksopp	So Easy
Bring Down The Birds	Herbie Hancock	Dee-Lite	Groove Is In The Heart
Bustin' Loose	Charles Brown	Nelly	Hot In Herre
Can You Feel It	The Jacksons	Tamperer feat. Maya	Feel It
Danube Incident	Lalo Schifrin	Portishead	Sour Times
Dream On	Aerosmith	Eminem	Sing For The Moment
Every Breath You Take	The Police	Puff Daddy	I'll Be Missing You
Free Fallin'	Tom Petty	De La Soul	Fallin'
Far Beyond	Locksmith	Basement Jaxx	Red Alert
Fate	Chaka Khan	Stardust	Music Sounds Better With You
Forget Me Nots	Patrice Rushen	George Michael	Fastlove
From Here To Eternity	Engelbert Humperdink	Kinobe	Slip Into Something More Comfortable
Good Times	Chic	Grandmaster Flash	Adventures On The Wheels Of Steel
Heartbeat	Taana Gardner	Ini Kamoze	Here Comes The Hot Stepper
He's Gonna Step On You Again	John Kangos	Happy Mondays	Step On
I Can't Write Left Handed	Bill Withers	Fatboy Slim feat. Macy Gray	Demons
I Found A Reason	Velvet Underground	Massive Attack	Risingson
I Got The…	Labi Siffre	Eminem	My Name Is

Original Song	Originally By	Sampled By	On
Ike's Rap II	Isaac Hayes	Portishead	Glory Box
Is It Love You're After	Rose Royce	S-Express	Theme From S-Express
It's Ecstasy	Barry White	Robbie Williams	Rock DJ
Jungle Boogie	Kool & The Gang	Madonna	Erotica
The Last Time	Rolling Stones	The Verve	Bitter Sweet Symphony
Liberian Girl	Michael Jackson	2Pac	Letter 2 My Unborn
Life In A Northern Town	Dream Academy	Dario G	Sunchyme
Love Action (I Believe In Love)	Human League	George Michael	Shoot The Dog
Love Is You	Carol Williams	Spiller	Groovejet (If This Ain't Love)
Love, Need And Want You	Patti LaBelle	Nelly feat. Kelly Rowland	Dilema
The Magic Number	Bob Dorough	De La Soul	The Magic Number
Make It Easy On Yourself	The Walker Brothers	Ash	Candy
Material Girl	Madonna	Tamperer feat. Maya	If You Buy This Record Your Life Will Be Better
Old Cape Cod	Patti Page	Groove Armada	At The River
Peter Piper	Run DMC	Missy Elliott	Work It
Shack Up Pt.1	Banbarra	Prince	Gett Off
Soup For One	Chic	Modjo	Lady
Stratus	Billy Cobham	Massive Attack	Safe From Harm
Superfreak	Rick James	MC Hammer	You Can't Touch This
Sway	Rosemary Clooney	Shaft	Mucho Mambo
Thank You	Dido	Eminem	Stan
Tramp	Lowell Fulson	Prince	7
Troubled So Hard	Vera Hall	Moby	Natural Blues
Try Again	Aaliyah	George Michael	Freeek!
Woman Of The Ghetto	Marlena Shaw	Blueboy	Remember Me
You Did It	Ann Robinson	Fatboy Slim	Gangsta Trippin'
The Young And Restless	Barry DeVorzon	Mary J. Blige	No More Drama

Samples 'Being Boiled' against vocals from 'Ain't Nobody' by Rufus & Chaka Khan

CHART ALBUMS WITH THE LONGEST ONE-WORD TITLES

TITLE	ARTIST	LETTERS
DECKSANDRUMSANDROCKANDROLL	Propellerheads	26
THEFAKESOUNDOFPROGRESS	Lostprophets	22
LABCABINCALIFORNIA	Pharcyde	18
SINGALONGAWARYEARS	Max Bygraves	18
SWORDFISHTROMBONES	Tom Waits	18
COOLEYHIGHHARMONY	Boyz II Men	17
AHUNDREDDAYSOFF	Underworld	15
BULLINAMINGVASE	Roy Harper	15
CALIFORNICATION	Red Hot Chili Peppers	15
INTERPRETATIONS	The Carpenters	15
LOVEHATETRAGEDY	Papa Roach	15
TROGGLODYNAMITE	The Troggs	15
BADMOTORFINGER	Soundgarden	14
BANDWAGONESQUE	Teenage Fanclub	14
DISINTEGRATION	The Cure	14
INDESTRUCTIBLE	Rancid	14
PHANTASMAGORIA	Curved Air/ The Damned	14
SINGALONGAXMAS	Max Bygraves	14
UNHALFBRICKING	Fairport Convention	14

CHART SINGLES WITH THE LONGEST ONE-WORD TITLES

TITLE	ARTIST	LETTERS
'ANOTHERLOVERHOLENYOHEAD'	Prince	23
'THEFAKESOUNDOFPROGRESS'	Lostprophets	22
'KLACTOVEESEDSTEIN'	Blue Rondo A La Turk	17
'DISCOBEATLEMANIA'	D.B.M.	16
'MISUNDERSTANDING'	Genesis	16
'(NONSTOPOPERATION)'	Dust Junkys	16

PRINCE

Song Lists

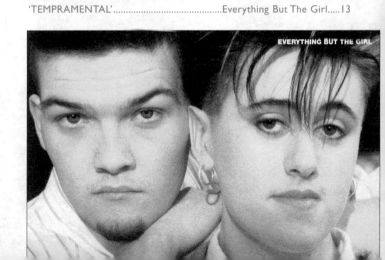

EVERYTHING BUT THE GIRL

MADNESS

THE FIRST NAME THEME

The subjects of these hits are so special, they don't even need a surname to identify them...

SONG	ARTIST	CHART POSITION	YEAR
'Diana'	Paul Anka	1	1957
'Fernando'	ABBA	1	1976
'Mandy'	Westlife	1	2003
'Maria'	Blondie	1	1999
'Stan'	Eminem	1	2000
'Vincent'	Don McLean	1	1972
'Denis (Denee)'	Blondie	2	1978
'Lola'	The Kinks	2	1970
'Mona'	Craig McLachlan	2	1990
'Eloise'	The Damned	3	1986
'Carrie'	Cliff Richard	4	1970
'Cecelia'*	Suggs	4	1996
'Daniel'	Elton John	4	1973
'Caroline'	Status Quo	5	1973
'Ben'	Michael Jackson	7	1972
'Jolene'	Dolly Parton	7	1976
'Layla'	Derek & The Dominos	7	1972
'Bernadette'	The Four Tops	8	1967
'Laura'	Scissor Sisters	10	2004
'Jacky'	Marc Almond	17	1991
'Adia'	Sarah McLachlan	18	1998
'Amanda'	Craig McLachlan	19	1990
'Valerie'	Steve Winwood	19	1987
'Jane'	Jefferson Starship	21	1980
'Lorraine'	Bad Manners	21	1980
'Christine'	Siouxsie & The Banshees	22	1980
'Isobel'	Björk	23	1995

*Originally recorded by Simon & Garfunkel

NAMED CHARACTERS

Here's a list of songs that have made it into the UK top 10
that are about named characters:

SONG	ARTIST	CHART POSITION	YEAR
'Annie's Song'	John Denver	1	1974
'Baby Jane'	Rod Stewart	1	1983
'Billie Jean'	Michael Jackson	1	1983
'Cathy's Clown'	The Everly Brothers	1	1960
'Eleanor Rigby'	The Beatles	1	1966
'Maggie May'	Rod Stewart	1	1971
'(Marie's The Name) His Latest Flame'	Elvis Presley	1	1961
'Oh, Julie'	Shakin' Stevens	1	1982
'Matthew And Son'	Cat Stevens	2	1967
'Barbara Ann'	The Beach Boys	3	1966
'Mary's Prayer'	Danny Wilson	3	1988
'A Boy Named Sue'	Johnny Cash	4	1969
'Dirty Diana'	Michael Jackson	4	1988
'Jesse Hold On'	B*Witched	4	1999
'Pictures Of Lily'	The Who	4	1967
'Dear Jessie'	Madonna	5	1989
'Jennifer Juniper'	Donovan	5	1968
'Nathan Jones'	The Supremes	5	1971
'See Emily Play'	Pink Floyd	6	1967
'Kevin Carter'	Manic Street Preachers	9	1996
'Oh Diane'	Fleetwood Mac	9	1982
'Lucy In The Sky With Diamonds'	Elton John	10	1974
'Martha's Harbour'	All About Eve	10	1988
'Sheila Take A Bow'	The Smiths	10	1987

Song Lists

TOP 20 RUDE SONG TITLES

Here's a collection of the rudest and crudest song titles ever!

'Leave This Off Your F**kin' Charts' ....Public Enemy

'I'll Shut Up When You F**k Off' ....Trigger Happy

'F**k Her Gently' ....Tenacious D

'Get Off My D*** And Tell Yo B****
To Come Here'...Ice Cube

'Such A T**t' ....The Streets

'Your Crutch F**kin' Stinks'............................Chaotic Dischord

'If You Don't Want To F**k Me Baby,
(Baby F**k Off)'....................Wayne Country & The Electric Chairs

'Mind F**kers F**king Mind' ....Flux Of Pink Indians

'C**try Pig'.......................................Lethal Agression

'We're F**kin' Glad The Smiths Split Up'...........Chaotic Dischord

'Too Drunk To F**k' (1)....................................Dead Kennedys

'F**k It (I Don't Want You Back)' (2) ....Eamon

'You're A F**king B****rd'....................................Exploited

'Hey Goth, F**k Off'..............................Chaotic Dischord

'Britain Is S**t' ....Selfish C**t

'Bunchof**kingoofs' ....Day Glo Abortions

'F**k Religion, F**k Politics,
And F**k The Lot Of You' ....Chaotic Dischord

'Nazi Punks F**k Off'..................................Dead Kennedys

'F**k Off!'...Kid Rock feat. Eminem

'F**k Me I'm Rich' ....Soundgarden

*(1) This song by the Dead Kennedy's was the
first song using the 'F' word to make it into the
British top 40.*

*(2) 'FURB (F U Right Back)' by Frankee
was released as a 'revenge' song to this
track by Eamon.*

Song Lists

EAMON

NAME CHECKS

This collection of famous people have all been immortalised into the titles of these classic songs:

'Bette Davies Eyes'..Kim Carnes
'Beethoven (I Love To Listen To)'......................................Eurythmics
'Bob Dylan's 115th Dream'..Bob Dylan
'Brian Wilson 2000'.......................................Barenaked Ladies
'Buddy Holly'...Weezer
'Calling Elvis'...Dire Straits
'Clint Eastwood'...Gorillaz
'Do It With Madonna'..Androids
'Elvis Presley And America'..U2
'Forget About Dre'..Eminem
'I Just Shot John Lennon'..The Cranberries
'James Dean (I Wanna Know)'.................Daniel Bedingfield
'Just Like Jesse James'...Cher
'Muhammad Ali'..Faithless
'Paul Newman's Eyes'......................................Dogs Die In Hot Cars
'Rasputin'...Boney M
'The Return Of Jimi Hendrix'.................................The Waterboys
'Robert De Niro's Waiting'...Bananarama
'Rock Me Amadeus'..Falco
'Roll Over Beethoven'..............................Electric Light Orchestra
'Sir Duke'..Stevie Wonder
'Star Spangled Banner Jimi Hendrix'..U2
'Thank You Jack White'....................................The Flaming Lips
'Tribute To Buddy Holly'...Mike Berry
'When Smokey Sings'...ABC

ELECTRIC LIGHT ORCHESTRA

LOU REED 'PERFECT DAY'
Number 1 1997 (19 weeks on chart).
BBC Children In Need cover version by Various Artists
A song about the relationship Reed had with heroin. A slightly
odd choice for a charity record...

AFROMAN 'BECAUSE I GOT HIGH'

AFROMAN

Number 1 2001 (15 weeks on chart).
Ten years ago, a record like this would
have been fit for a prestigious BBC ban,
although these days the BBC are far more
liberal with their attitude, and thanks to
being on the Radio 1 playlist, it hit the
top spot in 2001. This record however
could be viewed as an anti-drugs song,
as it demonstrates the oblivion and
repercussions caused by smoking
marijuana.

MUSICAL YOUTH 'PASS THE DUTCHIE'
Number 1 1982 (12 weeks on chart).
Based on 'Pass The Kutchie' by The Mighty
Diamonds. 'Kutchie' is a Jamaican word for a pipe of
marijuana. The British tabloids and broadcasting channels were
late to pick up on this, so the song avoided a ban, and reached
number 1.

THE SHAMEN 'EBENEEZER GOODE'
Number 1 1992 (10 weeks on chart).
At the height of the ecstasy club culture, this hit from
The Shamen caused a stir, resulting in a BBC ban, although the
band still insist that the song isn't about ecstasy. The song hit
number 1, although the negative publicity about it caused the
single to be pulled after four weeks.

MUSICAL YOUTH

THE STRANGLERS 'GOLDEN BROWN'
Number 2 1982 (12 weeks on chart).
Allegedly about heroin consumption,
although as the lyrics are so obscure the
song was never able to be banned.

D-MOB 'WE CALL IT ACIEEED'
Number 3 1988 (12 weeks on chart).
Another song banned by the BBC, this
tune hit the charts at the time of the 80s
ecstasy explosion, along with the smiley
yellow t-shirts and other paraphernalia.

THE BEATLES 'LUCY IN THE SKY WITH DIAMONDS'
Cover version by Elton John reached number 10 1974
(10 weeks on chart).
Just putting together the initials of the key words of this song
title gives the brand LSD, that along with a combination of the
Beatles psychedelic imagery, lyrics and admittance to taking 'tabs'
led to this song being tarred with the drug infused brush.

GRANDMASTER FLASH & MELLE MEL
'WHITE LINES (DON'T DO IT)'
Number 7 1984 (38 weeks on chart).
An anti-cocaine song written about the joys and resulting
dangers of the white powder, the song tells an important story
of how drug money serves negative parts of society.

PETER, PAUL & MARY 'PUFF THE MAGIC DRAGON'
Many people believe this is a song about drugs, although the
writers dispute this and claim it to be a song about childhood
innocence lost. Because of the many references to 'Puff', and the
place name, Hanah Lee, which apparently is really supposed to be
Hanalei, (an Hawaiian village famous for the greatness of its
drugs). The song got the pot smoking world excited with its
lyrics of 'autumn mist' and tenuous links to rolling papers…

JEFFERSON AIRPLANE 'WHITE RABBIT'
Based on the C S Lewis story *Alice In Wonderland* this song
is about having a hallucinogenic trip.

OTHER DRUG INDUCED SONGS

'Another Girl, Another Planet' .... The Only Ones
'Cocaine' .... Eric Clapton
'Cocaine' .... John Martyn
'Cold Turkey' .... John Lennon
'Eight Miles High' .... The Byrds
'Feel Good Hit Of The Summer' ...... Queens Of The Stone Age
'Here Comes The Nice' .... The Small Faces
'Heroin' .... Lou Reed
'Hits From The Bong' .... Cypress Hill
'Hurt' .... Johnny Cash/Nine Inch Nails
'I'm Waiting For The Man' .... The Velvet Underground
'The Needle And The .... Neil Young
Damage Done'
'Perfect Day' .... Lou Reed
'Purple Pills' D-12
'Rainy Day Women' .... Bob Dylan
'Under The Bridge' .... Red Hot Chili Peppers
'Weak Become Heroes' .... The Streets

TOP 20 SONGS ABOUT DRIVING

The ultimate driving compilation...

'Always Crashing In The Same Car' .. David Bowie
'Born To Be Wild' .... Steppenwolf
'Cars' .... Gary Numan
'Cars And Girls' .... Prefab Sprout
'Crash' .... The Primitives
'Drive' .... The Cars
'Drive' .... R.E.M.
'Drive My Car' .... The Beatles
'Fast Car' .... Tracy Chapman
'King Of The Road' .... Roger Miller

'No Particular Place To Go'	Chuck Berry
'The Passenger'	Iggy Pop
'Pink Cadillac'...	Natalie Cole
'Pull Up To The Bumper'.....................	Grace Jones
'Road To Nowhere'..............................	Talking Heads
'Road Trippin''	Red Hot Chili Peppers
'Roll On Down The Highway'	Bachman Turner Overdrive
'Rush Hour'...	Jane Wiedlin
'Take It Easy'	The Eagles

TOP 20 HEAVENLY SONGS

The following songs all reached the pearly gates of the UK top ten:

SONG	ARTIST	CHART POSITION	YEAR
'The Edge Of Heaven'	Wham!	1	1986
'Heaven'	DJ Sammy	1	2002
'Heaven Is A Place On Earth'	Belinda Carlisle	1	1987
'Outside Of Heaven'	Eddie Fisher	1	1953
'Show Me Heaven'	Maria McKee	1	1990
'Three Steps To Heaven'	Eddie Cochran	1	1960
'Heaven For Everyone'	Queen	2	1995
'Knockin' On Heaven's Door'	Guns N' Roses	2	1992
'Three Steps To Heaven'	Showaddywaddy	2	1975
'Heaven Must Have Sent You'	Elgins	3	1971
'Too Much Heaven'	The Bee Gees	3	1978
'Hands To Heaven'	Black	4	1988
'Heaven Is A Half Pipe'	OPM	4	2001
'Heaven Must Be Missing An Angel'	Tavares	4	1976
'Feels Like Heaven'	Urban Cookie Collective	5	1993
'Tears In Heaven'	Eric Clapton	5	1992
'(Feels Like) Heaven'	Fiction Factory	6	1984
'One Night In Heaven'	M People	6	1993
'And The Heavens Cried'	Anthony Newley	6	1961
'Stairway To Heaven'	Rolf Harris	7	1993

KISS

TOP 20 HELLISH SONGS

Those written about Hell, have barely scraped into the UK charts, here's 20 of the best...

'(As Long As They've Got) Cigarettes In Hell'	Oasis
'Bat Out Of Hell'	Meatloaf
'Better To Reign In Hell'	Cradle Of Filth
'Cold Day In Hell'	Gary Moore
'Facing Hell'	Ozzy Osbourne
'Good Day In Hell'	The Eagles
'Heaven & Hell'	Black Sabbath
'Heaven Or Hell'	The Stranglers
'Hell Hath No Fury'	Frankie Laine
'Hell Is Round The Corner'	Tricky vs. The Gravediggaz
'Hell Raiser'	Sweet
'The Hell Song'	Sum 41
'Hell's Party'	Glam
'Highway To Hell'	AC/DC
'Hotter Than Hell'	Kiss
'MF from Hell'	The Datsuns
'The Pretty Things Are Going To Hell'	David Bowie
'Private Hell'	The Jam
'The Road To Hell'	Chris Rea
'Straight To Hell'	The Clash

TOP 20 SONGS FROM THE MARKET STALL

The following songs all made it into the UK top 40.

SONG	ARTIST	CHART POSITION	YEAR
'Blackberry Way'	Move	1	1968
'Cherry Pink And Apple Blossom White'	Perez 'Prez' Prado	1	1955
'I Heard It Through 'The Grapevine'	Marvin Gaye	1	1969
'Banana Boat Song (Day-O)'	Harry Belafonte	2	1957
'Strawberry Fields Forever'	The Beatles	2	1967
'Banana Republic'	The Boomtown Rats	3	1980
'Clementine'	Mark Owen	3	1997
'Applejack'	Jet Harris & Tony Meehan	4	1963
'Strawberry Fair'	Anthony Newley	3	1960
'Strawberry Fields Forever'	Candy Flip	3	1990
'Blueberry Hill'	Fats Domino	6	1956
'Banana Splits (The Tra La La Song)'	Dickies	7	1979
'Green Onions'	Booker T And The MGs	7	1979
'Roobarb And Custard'	Shaft	7	1991
'Banana Boat Song'	Shirley Bassey	8	1957
'Big Apple'	Kajagoogoo	8	1983
'Clementine'	Bobby Darin	8	1980
'Here We Go Round The Mulberry Bush'	Traffic	8	1967
'Peaches'	Presidents Of The United States Of America	8	1996
'Onion Song'	Marvin Gaye	9	1969

KAJAGOOGOO

TOP 40 MOVIE SONGS

The following songs all made it to number 1 thanks to the film that they featured in. The 80s classic 'Ghostbusters' by Ray Parker Jnr only reached number 2 in the UK charts, but is worthy of a mention as it managed to stay on the charts for a lengthy 31 weeks in 1984. The one hit wonder 'Turtle Power' by Partners In Kryme, also made it to the top spot, but just missed inclusion on this list.

HUGH GRANT &
ANDIE MacDOWELL
FOUR WEDDINGS
AND A FUNERAL

FILM/ SONG	ARTIST	YEAR
FOUR WEDDINGS AND A FUNERAL		
'Love Is All Around'	Wet Wet Wet	1994
37 weeks on chart.		
G.I. BLUES		
'Wooden Heart'	Elvis Presley	1961
27 weeks on chart.		
GREASE		
'You're The One That I Want	John Travolta & Olivia Newton-John	1978
26 weeks on chart.		
ROBIN HOOD (PRINCE OF THIEVES)		
'(Everything I Do) I Do It For You'	Bryan Adams	1991
24 weeks on chart.		
THE WOMAN IN RED		
'I Just Called To Say I Love You'	Stevie Wonder	1984
24 weeks on chart.		

FILM/ SONG	ARTIST	YEAR

THE BODYGUARD
'I Will Always Love You' .... Whitney Houston 1992
23 weeks on chart.

EIGHT MILE
'Lose Yourself' .... Eminem 2002
21 weeks on chart.

SERIOUS CHARGE
'Living Doll' .... Cliff Richard 1959
21 weeks on chart.

DANGEROUS MINDS
'Gangsta's Paradise' .... Coolio 1995
20 weeks on chart.

TITANIC
'My Heart Will Go On' .... Celine Dion 1998
20 weeks on chart.

SATURDAY NIGHT FEVER
'Night Fever' .... The Bee Gees 1978
20 weeks on chart.

A MAN COULD GET KILLED
'Strangers In The Night' .... Frank Sinatra 1966
20 weeks on chart.

BREAKFAST AT TIFFANY'S
'Moon River' .... Danny Williams 1961
19 weeks on chart.

GREASE
'Summer Nights' .... John Travolta & 1978
19 weeks on chart. Olivia Newton-John

SUMMER HOLIDAY
'Summer Holiday' .... Cliff Richard 1963
18 weeks on chart.

COYOTE UGLY
'Can't Fight The Moonlight' .... LeAnn Rimes 2000
17 weeks on chart.

MANNEQUIN
'Nothing's Gonna Stop Us Now' .... Starship 1987
17 weeks on chart.

Song Lists

FRANK SINATRA

CHER

FILM/ SONG	ARTIST	YEAR

FAME
'Fame' ....Irene Cara 1982
16 weeks on chart.

MEN IN BLACK
'Men In Black'.................................Will Smith..1997
16 weeks on chart.

BUDDY'S SONG
'The One And Only' ....Chesney Hawkes 1991
16 weeks on chart.

THE BEACH
'Pure Shores' ....All Saints...2000
16 weeks on chart.

ROCKY III
'The Eye Of The Tiger'.................Survivor 1982
15 weeks on chart.

CHARLIE'S ANGELS
'Independent Women ....Destiny's Child................................2000
Part 1'
15 weeks on chart.

BRIDGET JONES'S DIARY
'It's Raining Men'...........................Geri Halliwell 2001
15 weeks on chart.

DONNIE DARKO
'Mad World' ....Michael Andrews 2003
15 weeks on chart.

MERMAIDS
'The Shoop ....Cher 1991
Shoop Song'
15 weeks on chart.

TOP GUN
'Take My Breath Away'.................Berlin..1986
15 weeks on chart.

NOTTING HILL
'When You Say ....Ronan Keating..................................1999
Nothing At All'
15 weeks on chart.

HELP!
'Help!' ....The Beatles..1965
14 weeks on chart.

FILM/ SONG	ARTIST	YEAR

DESPERATELY SEEKING SUSAN
'Into The Groove' ....Madonna 1985
14 weeks on chart.

JAILHOUSE ROCK
'Jailhouse Rock'.............................Elvis Presley....................1958
14 weeks on chart.

GIRLS, GIRLS, GIRLS
'Return To Sender' ....Elvis Presley 1962
14 weeks on chart.

DAYS OF THUNDER
'Show Me Heaven' ....Maria McKee 1990
14 weeks on chart.

GHOST
'Unchained Melody' ....Righteous Brothers 1990
14 weeks on chart.

A HARD DAY'S NIGHT
'A Hard Day's Night' ....The Beatles 1964
13 weeks on chart.

THE NEXT BEST THING
'American Pie' ....Madonna 2000
12 weeks on chart.

GODZILLA
'Deeper Underground'.................Jamiroquai.........................1998
11 weeks on chart.

LA BAMBA
'La Bamba'...............,....................Los Lobos 1987
11 weeks on chart.

STAND BY ME
'Stand By Me'................................Ben E. King 1987
11 weeks on chart.

SLIDING DOORS
'Turn Back Time' ....Aqua 1998
10 weeks on chart.

JAMIROQUAI

TOP 40 GREAT DUETS & COLLABORATIONS

For a variety of reasons, artists get together and record, some of them quite unexpectedly...

'Act Of War'	Elton John & Millie Jackson
'Against All Odds'	Westlife & Mariah Carey
'Baby It's Cold Outside'	Tom Jones & Cerys Matthews
'Don't Give Up'	Peter Gabriel & Kate Bush
'Gloria'	Van Morrison & John Lee Hooker
'Had To Be'	Cliff Richard & Olivia Newton John
'I Got You Babe'	Cher & Beavis & Butt-Head
'In A Lifetime'	Clannad feat. Bono
'Interlude'	Morrissey & Siouxsie
'Justified & Ancient'	The KLF feat. Tammy Wynette
'Lazy'	X-Press feat. David Byrne
'Live Like Horses'	Elton John & Luciano Pavarotti
'My Culture'	1 Giant Leap feat. Robbie Williams
'Never Be The Same Again'	Mel C & Lisa 'Left-Eye'Lopes
'Out In The Fields'	Gary Moore & Phil Lynott
'Peace On Earth/ Little Drummer Boy'	Bing Crosby & David Bowie
'Re-light My Fire'	Take That & Lulu
'Rise & Fall'	Craig David & Sting
'Say Say Say'	Paul McCartney & Michael Jackson
'Sex Bomb'	Tom Jones & Mousse T
'Scorpio Rising'	Liam Gallagher & Death In Vegas
'Signed, Sealed, Delivered I'm Yours'	Blue feat. Stevie Wonder & Angie Stone
'Silence'	Delirium feat. Sarah McLachlan

'Sisters Are Doing It For Themselves' .... Eurythmics & Aretha Franklin

'Some Velvet Morning' .... Primal Scream & Kate Moss

'Somethin' Stupid' .... Nicole Kidman & Robbie Williams

'Spirits In The Material World' .... Pato Banton & Sting

'This Is Not America' .... David Bowie & The Pat Metheny Group

'This Love' .... Craig Armstrong feat. Liz Fraser

'True Love Ways' .... Catherine Zeta Jones & David Essex

'U Got The Look' .... Prince & Sheena Easton

'Weather Storm' .... Massive Attack & Craig Armstrong

'Well, Did You Evah!' .... Deborah Harry & Iggy Pop

'What Have I Done To Deserve This' .... Pet Shop Boys feat. Dusty Springfield

'Whenever God Shines His Light' .... Van Morrison & Cliff Richard

'When Love Comes To Town' .... U2 & B. B. King

'Where Is My Boy' .... Faultline & Chris Martin

'Where The Wild Roses Grow' .... Nick Cave & Kylie Minogue

'Xanadu' .... Olivia Newton-John & Electric Light Orchestra

AROUND THE WORLD IN 40 SONGS

Compilations for the back-packer...

1	'Africa'	Toto
2	'America'	Simon & Garfunkel
3	'Antarctica'	Al Stewart
4	'Argentina'	Jeremy Healy & Amos
5	'Heart Of Asia'	Watergate
6	'Australia'	Manic Street Preachers
7	'Bedlam In Belgium'	AC/DC
8	'Bosnia'	The Cranberries
9	'The Brazilian'	Dirty Vegas
10	'England 2 Colombia 0'	Kirsty MacColl

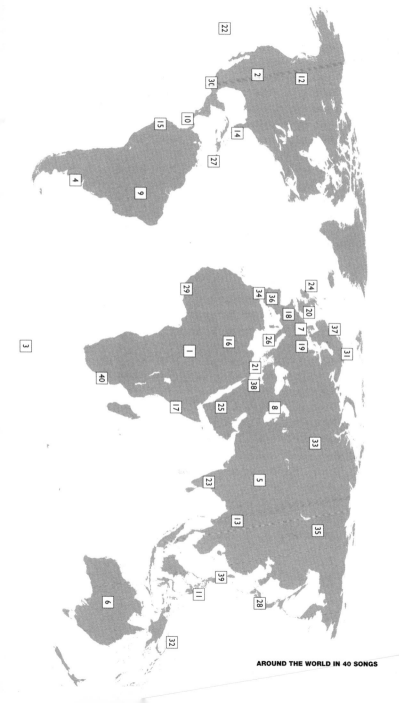

AROUND THE WORLD IN 40 SONGS

Song Lists

11 'Cambodia' .... Kim Wilde
12 'Blue Canadian Rockies' .... The Byrds
13 'China Girl' .... David Bowie
14 'Cuba' .... Gibson Brothers
15 'Ecuador' .... Sash! feat. Rodriguez
16 'Little Egypt' .... Elvis Presley
17 'Ethiopia' .... Joni Mitchell
18 'In France They Kiss On
Main Street' .... Joni Mitchell
19 'I'm In Love With A
German Film Star' .... The Passions
20 'Real Great Britain' .... Asian Dub Foundation
21 'Greece' .... George Harrison
22 'Walking 2 Hawaii' .... Tom McRae
23 'India' .... Roxy Music
24 'Give Ireland Back To The Irish' .. Paul McCartney
25 'Israel' .... Siouxsie & The Banshees
26 'Italian Girls' .... Rod Stewart
27 'Sweet Jamaica' .... Cat Stevens
28 'Japanese Boy' .... Aneka
29 'Liberian Girl' .... Michael Jackson
30 'Going To Mexico' .... Steve Miller Band
31 'Norwegian Wood' .... The Beatles
32 'Papua New Guinea' .... Future Sound Of London
33 'Poland' .... Tangerine Dream
34 'April In Portugal' .... Eartha Kitt
35 'Russians' .... Sting
36 'Spanish Harlem Incident' .... Bob Dylan
37 'Sweden' .... The Divine Comedy
38 'Cold Turkey' .... John Lennon
39 'Vietnam' .... Jimmy Cliff
40 'Zimbabwe' .... Bob Marley

SONGS FOR 40 CITIES

'Loco In Acapulco' .... The Four Tops
'Amsterdam' .... Coldplay
'Anchorage' .... Michelle Shocked

'Ballad Of The Bangkok Novotel' ..... Manic Street Preachers
'Barcelona'... Freddie Mercury &
Monserrat Caballe
'Belfast Child' ....,,,,,,, ... Simple Minds
'Boulder To Birmingham'.................... Emmylou Harris
'Night Boat To Cairo' .... Madness
'Take Me Back To Chicago'................ Chigaco
'El Paso' .... Marty Robins
'Harlem In Havana' .... Joni Mitchell
'Hong Kong Garden'........................... Siouxsie & The Banshees
'Jerusalem'.. Emerson, Lake & Palmer
'Katmandu'.. Cat Stevens
'Kingston Town' UB40
'Viva Las Vegas' .... Elvis Presley
'Leningrad'.. Billy Joel
'Long Haired Lover From
Liverpool'.. Jimmy Osmond
'London Calling' .... The Clash
'Te Dejo Madrid' .... Skakira
'Memphis Tennessee' .... Status Quo
'Radio Moscow'.................................... Moloko
'Nashville Skyline Rag'........................ Bob Dylan
'Queen Of New Orleans'.................. Jon Bon Jovi
'New York' .... Ryan Adams
'Panama'... Van Halen
'Paris Four Hundred'.......................... Mylo
'Philadelphia Freedom' .... Elton John
'Portsmouth'... Mike Oldfield
'Rio'.. Duran Duran
'Rome Wasn't Built In A Day'........... Morcheeba
'Rotterdam'... The Beautiful South
'Miss Sarajevo' ,,,,, ... U2
'Shanghai'd In Shanghai'..................... Nazareth
'Stockholm Syndrome' .... Muse
'Life In Tokyo' .... Japan
'Vancouver' .... Jeff Buckley
'Sink Venice' .... Ikara Colt
'Vienna'.. Ultravox
'Warsaw'.. Joy Division

A classic song for every day of the week...

'Blue Monday' .... New Order
'Ruby Tuesday' .... The Rolling Stones
'Wednesday Morning 3am' .... Simon & Garfunkel
'Thursday's Child'................................ David Bowie
'Friday I'm In Love' .... The Cure
'Saturday Sun' .... Nick Drake
'Sunday Bloody Sunday'...................... U2

Chapter 7
Music Festivals

The UK music festival scene is at its biggest and best right now!
Here's where it all began...

MONTEREY POP FESTIVAL

16-18 June 1967, Montery, California. Featuring performances
by The Animals, The Byrds, Buffalo Springfield, Canned Heat, Jimi
Hendrix, Janis Joplin, Scot McKenzie, The Mamas and Papas, Otis
Redding, Ravi Shankar, Simon & Garfunkel, The Who and many
more. Over 10,000 people gathered around the Monterey
County grounds for the three day festival. The event is generally
regarded as the beginning of the 'summer of love'.

The event was filmed by D.A. Pennebaker, who captured the
performances on celluloid. It was the first American performing
experience for The Who and Jimi Hendrix, and provided major
exposure for artists like Janis Joplin and Otis Redding. The DVD
of the event is still available to buy.

Most of the performers appeared for free, and funds raised
by the festival and subsequent film and CD releases go to the
Monterey Pop Foundation, which is still raising money today.

WOODSTOCK

WOODSTOCK MUSIC FESTIVAL

15-17 August 1969 USA. The Woodstock Music & Art festival
is seen as the most legendary rock concert of all time. Over
400,000 people turned up to Max Yusgur's dairy farm near the
village of Bethel, around 50 miles from the town of Woodstock.
Tickets were $18.

Music Festivals

The festival cost somewhere in the region of $2.4m to put on, and was sponsored by four young Americans, John Roberts, Joel Rosenman, Artie Kornfeld and Michael Lang. All four men had separate, but similar ideas about holding some sort of musical extravaganza, and when all four met the idea of Woodstock was born, although they still disagree as to who came up with the original idea for the festival.

Billed as 'Three days of peace and music', the festival was the highlight of the 'hippie era', where attendees spent three days celebrating peace, love, rock and roll and the rest...

Amongst those performing were Jimi Hendrix, Janis Joplin, The Who, Santana, The Grateful Dead, The Band and Ravi Shankar.

In 1970 a documentary film of the festival was released. Directed by Michael Wadleigh, and edited by Martin Scorsese, the film *Woodstock* won an Academy Award for Best Documentary Feature, and is an important record of the performances and atmosphere of the festival.

In 1994 an anniversary Woodstock festival was held featuring acts such as Green Day and Nine Inch Nails. In July 1999 a third anniversary concert was held in New York with tickets on sale for $150, with Limp Bizkit and Korn performing, amongst others. For this event it seemed as if the original Woodstock ethic had been totally lost in the new generation of music fans, as there were riots, fires and rape allegations.

WOODSTOCK 1969

GLASTONBURY

Held annually in Somerset, UK (1970 – present day). The first Glastonbury festival was organised on September 19 & 20, 1970 by Michael and Jean Eavis at Worthy Farm, Pilton, near Glastonbury, Somerset. They had been inspired by the nearby Bath Blues festival, and decided to organise a two day event on their own land. The entrance fee was £1 which included free milk! Around 1,500 people turned up to watch acts such as Al Stewart, Marc Bolan & T Rex, Quintessence and local blues and folk bands. Eavis predicted making a profit, but ended up making a loss of £1,500.

1971 saw the first "legendary" Glastonbury and a temporary Pyramid Stand was erected. Acts included David Bowie, Joan Baez, Fairport Convention and Hawkwind. The festival was free of charge for the 12,000 attendees, funded by rich hippies such as Arabella Churchill (who is still involved in the festival today) and Andrew Kerr. There was no alcohol on sale and all the food was vegetarian.

Between 1972 and 1979 no festivals were held, although thousands of hopefuls still turned up at the site.

The 1979 Glastonbury festival was the first officially "commercial" three day event. Tickets were £5, and all profit went to the UN Year of the Child, which helped found the Children's World charity. Headline acts included Genesis, Peter Gabriel and Tom Robinson.

The 1981 event Eavis sees as the "breakthrough" festival. The audience doubled in size with 24,000 attending, and an £8 entrance fee raised money for the Campaign for Nuclear Disarmament (CND), which was to become a popular beneficiary of the festival.

MICHAEL EAVIS

GLASTONBURY CAMPSITE

A permanent Pyramid Stage was built, doubling up as a cow shed for the rest of the year! New Order, Hawkwind and Aswad were the main acts.

In 1982 U2, Van Morrison, The Thompson Twins and Jackson Browne performed.

1983 saw the launch of Radio Avalon, the festival's official radio station. It was also the first year that required a festival licence after a new law was introduced by a local MP. Attendance was limited to 30,000, and there were performances from UB40, Marillion and The Cheiftans. Ticket prices increased to £12.

The Green Field was introduced in 1984, mainly to accommodate new-age travellers. This year featured The Waterboys, The Smiths, Fela Kuti and Elvis Costello, the entry fee was £13.

Eavis had purchased an extra 100 acres of land in 1985 to cope with more people, but despite the agreed 60,000 limit over 100,000 people attended. Artists included Boomtown Rats, The Pogues, The Style Council and Hugh Masekela.

In 1986 the local council refused Eavis a licence for the first time, due to going over the agreed attendance limit the year before. Eavis took them to court and won. 60,000 attended paying £17 to watch acts such as The Cure, Madness, Simply Red and Psychedellic Furs.

The council and local villagers were against the festival again in 1987, but Eavis managed to overturn the initial licence refusal. Drug taking became an issue, resulting in the cancellation of the 1988 festival. The WOMAD stage was introduced for the first year, and attendees paid £21 to see performances from Julian Cope, New Order, Courtney Pine and Van Morrison amongst others.

In 1989 police patrolled the festival for the first time (previous festivals had had on-site security). £100,000 is raised for CND and ticket prices are increased to £28. Suzanne Vega, Pixies and Wonderstuff are some of the performers.

The 1990 festival saw a number of fights resulting in £50,000 damage, which led to the cancellation of the 1991 festival. 70,000 attended, watching The Cure, Happy Mondays, and Ry Cooder amongst others. This is the last festival for which CND receive funding from the festival as the Cold War comes to an end. This was also the year Glastonbury officially became The Glastonbury Festival of Contemporary Performing Arts.

In 1992 the festival managed to raise £250,000 for Oxfam and Greenpeace. The ticket price was now £49 with performances from Primal Scream, PJ Harvey, Blur and The Fall.

The 1993 festival had an increased licence for 80,000 people and ticket prices had increased by a third since 1990 to £58. Featured artists included Lenny Kravitz, Jamiroquai and Suede.

1994 saw the first ever Glastonbury fatality, where a man died from a drugs overdose. Five people were also injured when a gunman opened fire. The entrance fee was now £59, and headline acts included Björk, Orbital and the Manic Street Preachers.

In 1995, after tickets had sold out in record time, the site fencing was pulled down, making the festival a free event for many lucky visitors, and over 80,000 people attended. This year also was the first to see the dance tent.

The 1997 festival was over-shadowed by bad weather, turning the 800 acres into a mud bath. Radiohead, Supergrass and Sting headlined.

In 1999 the festival cost £83 to get in and had more acts than ever before, with performances from R.E.M., Muse, David Gray and Skunk Anansie.

The 2000 festival featured David Bowie, Moby, Macy Gray and Muse, but too many people gate-crashed, resulting in the cancellation of the 2001 festival.

A £1m "super-fence" was erected in 2002 and since then the festival organisers have maintained a strict 'no ticket, no entry' policy. Eavis collaborated with the Mean Fiddler group to help with security and organisation. The ticket fee was now £100, and headline acts included Coldplay, Stereophonics, Rod Stewart and The White Stripes.

Now costing a massive £105, the 2003 festival sold out in 24 hours, with fans desperate to see R.E.M., Radiohead, The Polyphonic Spree and The Flaming Lips perform.

2004 was another successful sold out event, with Paul McCartney, Oasis, Muse, Kings Of Leon and Keane amongst the main acts.

The 2005 event sold out again in a matter of hours with the lure of acts such as Coldplay, Bloc Party, The Killers and Rufus Wainwright tempting music fans. Ticket prices are now £125. There will be no festival in 2006.

GLASTONBURY NOW

Glastonbury is the largest Greenfield music and performing arts festival.

In 2004 over 112,000 tickets were sold within 24 hours of going on sale. The official ticket website had over two million hits. 2,500 people phoned the ticket sales telephone number a minute.

As well as the 112,500 visitors, the performers and crew make up another 34,000 people.

The festival site today occupies 900 acres of land. The entertainment area is 1.5 miles across, with an 8.5 mile perimeter. The site is surrounded by a 6.9km long, 3.6m high fence.

Over three million gallons of water are used during each festival. More than 250,000 bottles of water are consumed. Over £1 million has been raised for WaterAid.

Around 2,000 performers play on over 25 stages, which include cabaret, theatre, circus and poetry readings. There is also an on-site cinema. 700,000 gallons of human waste are produced during the festival in the 2,500 camp toilets.

Around 400,000 pints of beer are consumed, with 1000 bar staff in 18 bars, all supplied by 40 tankers.

There are 17 different market areas with a total of 687 stalls.

120,000 bin-liners, 1000 recycle drums, 4500 painted waste bins were used in 2003. A team of 1100 recycling and litter-picking staff help to keep the festival as clean as possible.

OTHER FESTIVALS

THE BIG CHILL
Was founded in 1994, and began as an all day Sunday event in London. Increasing annually in size, it is now a three day festival held near Malvern in Herefordshire, UK. The festival is well regarded as being a multi-media event, with the focus being on new music, and also has its own record company and a bar.

HOMELANDS
Held near Winchester, Hampshire, Homelands is the first major UK music festival of the summer. Focussing on dance music, the event lasts just for one day and attracts around 35, 000 people.

163

FESTIVAL IN THE DESERT

This world music festival ('Festival au Désert'), began in 2001, and is becoming increasingly popular. Held annually for three days in Essakane in Mali, (you can only reach the festival by camel-back, or in a 4x4) the festival is open to musicians from all over the world, as well as encouraging dance, poetry and traditional song, as a key point to the festival is to maintain the time-honoured culture of the area.

THE ISLE OF WIGHT ROCK FESTIVAL

The first festival was held in 1968, with an estimated 10,000 people watching acts such as Jefferson Airplane, The Move and Fairport Convention. Tickets were sold at a measly £1.25! In 1969 the festival had doubled in size, with the major acts being Bob Dylan, Joe Cocker, The Band and The Moody Blues. The festival in 1970 was so enormous (attracting an estimated 600,000 music fans) that an 'Isle Of Wight Act' was passed in 1971, which required organised gatherings of over 5,000 people to have a licence. There were to be no more festivals until 2002, when the Isle Of Wight Festival was resurrected, and have continued yearly since then.

READING & LEEDS
CARLING MUSIC FESTIVAL

The Reading Festival originated in the 1960s under the name 'The National Jazz & Blues Festival', which later moved towards rock and roll music, and was where The Rolling Stones appeared in 1963, and at the first three day event in 1964. During the 70s the festival was rock orientated, with bands such as Thin Lizzy, Status Quo and AC/DC performing. In 1992 Nirvana headlined, this was to be their last UK live performance.

Over the years the festival has grown, and in 1999 launched a sister festival based in Leeds. In 2004 the headline acts included The Darkness, The White Stripes and Morrissey. With The Killers, Pixies, Foo Fighters and Iron Maiden headlining 2005.

V FESTIVALS

Sponsored by Virgin (hence the 'V'), the festival is held in two locations in the UK, Chelmsford and Staffordshire, with the bands playing at the festival swapping venues each day.

JAMELIA PERFORMS AT THE 'V FESTIVAL', CHELMSFORD, ENGLAND, 21 AUGUST 2004

WOMAD

Standing for World Of Music Arts and Dance, Womad is a world-wide music festival celebrating artists from all over the world. Originally inspired by Peter Gabriel in 1982, there are now annual festivals in Reading (UK), Cornwall (UK), Adelaide (Australia), Cáceres (Spain), Taormina (Sicily), Singapore and the Canary Islands.

PETER GABRIEL

Music Festivals

Chapter 8
Sound & Recording

SOUND & RECORDING FACTS

The first sound recording to be made on a machine was 'Mary Had A Little Lamb'. This was recorded on December 6th, 1877 by Thomas Edison.

The first juke-box was installed at Palais Royal Hotel in San Francisco, November 23rd, 1890.

HMV recorded the first complete opera in 1903, Verdi's *Ernani*, which was made up of 40 single sided discs.

The first recording to coin the term "album" was Tchaikovsky's *Nutcracker Suite* which was released on four double sided discs in 1909. It reminded people of a photo album…

The first jazz record was released in 1917 by the Dixieland Jass Band with the songs 'Livery Stable Blues' and 'Dixie Jass Band One Step'.

The first LP was developed by Thomas Edison in 1926. It was 12 inches in diameter, and one and a half inches thick, weighed two pounds and was played with a diamond stylus.

EMI set up Abbey Road Studios in 1931, which was the largest recording studio in the world at that time

ABBEY ROAD STUDIOS

The first recorded song called 'Rock And Roll' was by the Boswell Sisters in 1934.

The first 45 rpm record was released by RCA in 1949. The first song to top the charts on this format was 'A - You're Adorable' by Perry Como.

The first use of an echo chamber on a recording was in 1950 on 'Foolish Heart' by Junior Mance, where a boom mike was used in a bathroom.

The first eight track recorder was built by Les Paul in 1954.

Philips introduced the first compact radio cassette in 1963.

The first British pirate radio broadcast was in 1964 by Radio Caroline. The station started broadcasting from the ex-passenger ferry MV Fredericia, anchored in international waters three miles off the Essex coast of south east England, and quickly became the most popular radio station in the UK.

The Grateful Dead produced 'Wall Of Sound' in 1974 which was the first recording to incorporate separate systems for vocals, each guitar, piano and drums.

The first picture disc (7") was 'Hold The Line' by Toto, released in 1979.

SOUND & RECORDING FORMATS

The first major recording companies (Columbia in 1889, and RCA and Decca following soon after), were highly competitive in a new industry of recording sound, and improving technology.

By the 1930s, the ten-inch 78rpm shellac disc was the standard format, although the record companies were still battling to improve the sound quality.

In 1948 Columbia released the twelve inch 33⅓ rpm LP, (long player) using a newly developed vinyl.

RCA, in response to this format, then developed the 7 inch vinyl, which played at 45 rpm. Eventually the two companies would merge their products, and agreed to produce records in both formats. It became the norm for classical records to be on LPs, and popular singles to be on 45s.

Vinyl was the market leader until the end of the 1980s, when the cassette tape was outselling records by three to one. Cassettes were introduced in the mid 1960s, and were popular because of their compact, small size.

The cassette tape created new popular music cultures. The portability of the cassette tape helped to mould the inner-city youth music scenes, a prime example being break-dancing, where portable stereos were taken onto the streets, creating new forms of social and street culture.

The tape also started the problems of illegal copying, as now you could record music from the radio and tape-to-tape. The home mix tape compilation became very fashionable in the 80s & 90s.

CDs (Compact Discs) are 4.5 inch discs, and in the 1980s established themselves as the main medium of recorded music. The idea of a disc was initially proposed in 1978 by Philips.

The CD was developed by Sony and Philips, and CDs began to be mass produced in 1982. By 1990 28% of all US households owned a CD player.

The CD format encouraged record companies to re-release their back catalogue to a whole new generation of listeners. It also became the trend to re-master the original recordings, and to add bonus tracks and special features on the CD. The boxed set also became popular, and for the first time fans could buy an artists complete recordings in a box.

Sound & Recording

Development of the MP3 (Moving Picture Expert Group Level 3) format started in Germany, 1987 at the Fraunhofer Institut, and in the late 90s there was a dramatic increase in its popularity,

The MP3 was developed by Karlheinz Brandenburg who began experimenting with compressing music in 1977. By 1997 he had a format which was a compressed WAV file, where the listener couldn't tell the difference in the audio quality.

The MP3 has changed the music industry dramatically, as now there was a format which allowed high quality music to be transferred over the internet and streamed directly into home computers. It also caused music piracy to be at an all time high, especially with the launch of Napster and other MP3 sharing applications. A new revolution of music sharing was born.

The first track to be made into an MP3 was 'Tom's Diner' by Suzanne Vega. This song was chosen because it is a quiet track, and therefore easier to pick up faults.

Today, the iPOD MP3 player is one of the most popular accessories, and has helped the download market to boom.

POP MUSIC ON TV

In 1952 the BBC launched **Hit Parade**. On the show songs were performed by a team of resident musicians (led by Petula Clark), rather than the original artists.

The BBC broadcast **Off The Record** in 1955 featuring pop news and interviews.

ITV began broadcasting **TV Music Shop** also in 1955.

PETULA CLARK

December 1956 **Cool For Cats** was launched. This was a 15 minute programme where records were played, and commented on. This ran until 1959.

In 1957 the BBC broadcast **Six-Five Special** which was aimed at younger viewers, and featured live music with a live audience.

ITV began **Oh Boy!** in 1958 in direct competition with **Six-Five Special**, featuring non-stop music. Cliff Richard appeared on the first show, helping him to enter the charts two weeks later with the single 'Move It'.

In January 1959 **Dig This** replaced **Six-Five Special**, although the show was dropped two months later, and replaced by **Drumbeat** which launched the career of Adam Faith. **Juke Box Jury** replaced **Drumbeat** in August 1959.

Boy Meets Girl replaced **Oh Boy!** in September 1959.

Thank Your Lucky Stars was first shown in April 1961 intended to rival **Juke Box Jury**. On January 19th, 1963, The Beatles made their first networked TV performance on the show, with a performance of 'Please Please Me'. The Rolling Stones also made their UK TV debut in 1963 miming to 'Come On'. **Thank Your Lucky Stars** ran for five years.

The BBC launched **Top Of The Pops** on January 1st, 1964. It was broadcast from a converted church in Manchester, and originally commissioned for only six shows. Introduced by Jimmy Saville, The Rolling Stones opened the show with 'I Wanna Be Your Man'. This first show also featured Dusty Springfield, Dave Clarke Five, The Hollies, The Swinging Blue Jeans, Cliff Richard & The Shadows, Freddie & The Dreamers and The Beatles who performed their current number 1, 'I Want To Hold Your Hand'. **Top Of The Pops** has since produced almost 2000 shows.

ADAM FAITH

STATUS QUO *TOP OF THE POPS* 1968

In April 1968 Pan's People were introduced to be the resident dancers on **Top Of The Pops**. The troupe would dance to the record when an artist couldn't appear on the show themselves. Pan's People danced on the shows until April 1976, with Legs & Co. eventually replacing them.

The Old Grey Whistle Test was another BBC music show which ran from 1971–1987. This was the first British programme to air a performance by Bob Marley & The Wailers.

MTV first went on air in the US on 1st August 1981, with 'Video Killed The Radio Star' by Buggles being the first video played. MTV was the first non-stop music video channel, and its launch marked a new era in pop music. MTV launched MTV Europe in 1987 which brought millions more viewers. MTV today describes itself as "the biggest youth broadcaster in the world".

173

JOOLS HOLLAND
& PAULA YATES

In 1982, Channel 4 broadcast a new music show called
The Tube, which was presented by Jools Holland, Terry Christian
and Paula Yates, and was an excellent showcase for many up and
coming bands of the time.

Later With Jools Holland began in 1992 and is still aired on the BBC. The show features a number of live bands, and customarily has a jam session at the start of the show with Jools Holland and all the invited guests playing together.

THE ELECTRIC GUITAR STORY

George Beauchamp and John Dopyera, musicians from Los Angeles, experimented with creating a louder guitar in the 1920s. They created a Hawaiian guitar with a horn attached to the bottom, however, the sound was terrible.

Beauchamp & Dopyera formed a new company in 1927 and patented the resonator guitar, which became very popular amongst slide blues guitarists.

In the early 1930s Beauchamp designed a guitar pick-up by using two horseshoe magnets and small pole pieces.

'The Frying Pan' was the first electric guitar to be made by Harry Watson in 1932. It was a Hawaiian style instrument made from one solid piece of hollowed out aluminium.

1933 saw the creation of the first electric Spanish guitar, made by Lloyd Loar, who worked for the Gibson guitar company. The pick-up however, created a fuzzy, distorted sound.

By 1935 Gibson had created a more successful pick-up, which produced a clean, full sound. This pick-up was put on all Gibson Hawaiian guitars.

At the same time, Gibson put out a Spanish guitar, the ES-150, which was a jazz guitar, with a unique design feature – the tremolo arm, which created a vibrato effect. Gibson guitars were far from perfect however, and the guitarist had to deal with problems of feedback, distortion and overtones.

Guitarist Les Paul managed to overcome these problems, and designed a new pick-up for a new jazz guitar nicknamed 'The Log'.

Sound & Recording

THE 'LOG'

Leo Fender developed a new guitar in 1943, and built what would become the first successful solid body guitar. Initially this was named the 'Esquire', then the 'Broadcaster' and finally the 'Telecaster'. This instrument however, was a guitar suited to the rock 'n' roll genre, so became most popular in the 50s and 60s.

1952 saw great developments in the solid-body electric guitar. The new guitar bore Les Paul's name, but the actual design for the guitar came from the new president of Gibson,

Ted McCarty.

In 1954 Fender introduced the Stratocaster which became the essential instrument for blues and rock players.

In 1958 Ted McCarty started designing futuristic guitars that would only become successful when heavy metal music became popular in the 70s and 80s. The Les Paul SG (Solid Guitar), made in 1961 became a vital tool for rock musicians such as Pete Townsend (The Who) and Toni Tommi (Black Sabbath).

LES PAUL SG (SOLID GUITAR)

Chapter 9
Music Genre Definitions

AMBIENT

This is a style of 'new age' music, which has really found its niche in the last two decades, although it has its roots in the 1970s. Generally, the music is minimal, hypnotic, made up of subtle beats and smooth musical themes. Often the pieces are long and predominantly instrumental. In the 1970s, Brian Eno was a key figure in developing the ambient style, producing albums such as *Ambient 1 – Music For Airports* (1978), which is regarded as a classic in this genre.

Listening Guide:
Aphex Twin *Selected Ambient Works Vol. II* (1994), Biosphere *Substrata* (1997), The Orb *U.F.Orb* (1992), Future Sound Of London *Lifeforms* (1994).

ART ROCK/PROGRESSIVE ROCK

Beginning in the late 60s, art/'prog' rock fused jazz and classical music with rock, was written free from the constraints of tempo, time, form and harmony and often had literary themes that were obscure, psychedelic and fantastical. The pieces were rarely less than seven minutes, and the themes would be constantly evolving, with unexpected combinations of instruments, like church organ with electric guitar for example. Prog. rock bands would often put on extravagant shows, a classic being Rick Wakeman's *Myths And Legends Of King Arthur* (1975), where there were 50 knights on hobby horses, 50 damsels, a massive orchestra with choir, a seven piece rock band, a narrator, a castle as the scenery, and all this was performed on ice!

Listening Guide:
King Crimson *In The Court Of The Crimson King* (1969), Jethro Tull *A Passion Play* (1972), Pink Floyd *Dark Side Of The Moon* (1973), Genesis *Wind And Wuthering* (1977).

RICK WAKEMAN

JETHRO TULL

DISCO

Made into a popular dance cult genre after the success of the film *Saturday Night Fever*, disco hit its peak in the 70s/80s (with thanks to the club Studio 54). Often distinguishable by a bass line hook and driving four-to-the-floor beat, disco also borrowed from funk and soul and was particularly popular on the gay scene.

Listening Guide:
Various Artists *Saturday Night Fever* (1977), Chic 'C'est Chic' (1979), Sister Sledge 'We Are Family' (1979), ABBA *Gold* (1992).

DOWNTEMPO/CHILLOUT/LEFTFIELD

These are related to the ambient style, but are more generally blends of ambient, new jazz, dub, acoustic, soul and electronica. This laid back style of music serves a function as background music ideal for socialising, rather than being dance floor records, although there is an element of cross over with many downtempo tunes being remixed for the club scene.

Listening Guide:
Kinobe 'Slip Into Something More Comfortable' (from *Soundphiles*) (2000), Mr Scruff 'Midnight Feast' (from *Keep It Unreal*) (1999), Zero 7 *Distractions* (2001), Bonobo *Dial M For Monkey* (2003).

ELECTRO

Electro is an early form of electronica, although more structured and closer to disco and funk, and has had heavy influences on the house, techno, synth-pop styles to come. Kraftwerk are seen as the pioneers of electro music, they introduced new techniques and new ways to use electronic equipment.

Listening Guide:
Kraftwerk *Autobahn* (1975), Afrika Bambaataa 'Planet Rock' (1982).

KRAFTWERK

ELECTRONICA

(Folktronica)

An ambiguous term that has been used since the 1960s when Stockhausen and Cage were experimenting, to describe electronic music that is not specifically designed for the dance floor, nor strictly chillout! The music is often quite experimental sounding, and uses a variety of beats and custom made electronic sounds. The themes often incorporate many musical genres, including classical, folk and jazz. More recently groups such as Four Tet have been given the description 'folktronica', which refers to their choice of instrumentation and melodies.

Listening Guide:
Felix Da Housecat *Kittenz And Thee Glitz* (2001), Four Tet *Rounds* (2003), Röyksopp *Melody AM* (2002).

JAMES BROWN

FUNK

A combination of jazz, soul and swing, funk came from a predominantly black culture, and made a massive contribution to the birth of disco, pop, hip hop and jungle music (James Brown's 'Funky Drummer' is one of the most sampled drum loops in hip hop and drum 'n' bass). Funk is characterised by syncopated rhythms coming from a large percussion section, a hook bass line, interjections of brass and electric guitar, and strong vocals. Prince and Jamiroquai have both helped carry funk into the 21st century.

Listening Guide:
James Brown *The Godfather – The Very Best Of James Brown* (2002), Earth Wind And Fire *Boogie Wonderland – The Best Of Earth Wind And Fire* (1996).

GLAM ROCK

At its peak in the 1970s, glam rock had its own particular style thanks to the flamboyancy of the likes of David Bowie, Marc Bolan and Gary Glitter. Rather than being defined specifically by the music, glam rock also describes the heavy make-up and outrageous clothes worn by the artists. It was imagery based, and bands such as Queen managed to fuse glam with progressive and art rock.

Listening Guide:
David Bowie *The Rise & Fall Of Ziggy Stardust And The Spiders From Mars* (1972), T Rex *Prophets Seers & Sages The Angels Of The Ages/My People Were Fair* (1972), Gary Glitter *Glitter* (1972).

DAVID BOWIE

GOTHIC ROCK

Like glam rock, there is a distinctive imagery in gothic rock, usually defined by wild black hair, dark eye make-up, powdered white faces and red lips. The clothing was all black, and slightly unkempt. The artists were often angst ridden, and combined fairly drone like vocals with catchy guitar riffs and occasional use of synths. The music came out of the punk movement.

Listening Guide:
The Cure *Standing On A Beach – The Singles* (1986), Siouxsie & The Banshees *Kaleidoscope* (1980).

HIP HOP/RAP

(Gangsta Rap/Hardcore Rap/East Coast)
The hip hop scene came out of the black street culture primarily in New York, along with breakdancing, graffiti, clothing, MCing and DJing. Much of the style comes from dub reggae, and then the artists began speaking in sync (street poetry/ storytelling) with percussive rhythms (MCing/rapping).
In the early days DJs would play records of many genres, and MCs would improvise in rap over the top. This also led to the 'turntablism' genre which incorporates scratching and beat juggling records. Many of the early rappers cut out the middle man by signing to independent record labels, and later the style was picked up by the major labels and also white artists.

Listening Guide:
Grandmaster Flash & The Furious Five *Back To The Old School* (1999), Sugarhill Gang 'Rapper's Delight' (1979), De La Soul *3 Feet High And Rising* (1989).

GRAND MASTER FLASH

187

HOUSE
(Hard House/Deep House/Acid House/
Progressive House/Tribal)

Another form of electronic music, house music has created much of the Western club scene. It is generally a four-four beat generated by a drum machine, with a solid bass. Often samples and looped vocals are used from all musical genres, notably soul, funk and jazz. House music is often of a similar BPM (beats per. minute, with Deep House being slightly slower) so mixing the tunes together is easier. Many different genres of house music are based on a particular electronic instrument, i.e. a specific drum machine with particular sounds. The house music scene is also heavily into remixing pop acts, so there are many 'house' remixes of Madonna, Kylie and even U2.

Listening Guide:
A Guy Called Gerald 'Voodoo Ray' (1989), Frankie Knuckles *Your Love* (1989), Shapeshifters 'Lola's Theme' (2004), Mylo *Destroy Rock And Roll* (2004).

JUNGLE/DRUM 'N' BASS
(Ragga Jungle/Oldskool/Jazz Step)
Hip-hop breaks and speeded up samples over dub/reggae bass lines create these styles, resulting in their notorious frantic sound, and very deep bass. Both jungle and drum 'n' bass borrow heavily from many other genres, and with the use of loops, and ability to speed everything up electronically can put old music into a totally new context. The style is in many ways defined by the use of the break-beat, which is a beat, often played on the off-beat between 160-180 beats per minute over the top of an irregular bass line, which differentiates it from other forms of dance music.

GOLDIE

Music Genre Definitions

Listening Guide:
Ronnie Size & Reprazent *New Forms* (1997), Goldie *Inner City Life* (1996), Squarepusher *Do You Know Squarepusher* (2002).

NU SOUL

This genre is a combination of R 'n' B, soul and hip hop, often using the vocal acrobatics of soul music, but with a hip hop beat and R 'n' B style instrumentation. The genre became particularly popular in the late 90s with artists such as Alicia Keys, Lauryn Hill and Mary J. Blige being the fore-runners.

Listening Guide:
Lauryn Hill *The Miseducation Of Lauryn Hill* (1998), D'Angelo *Voodoo* (2000), Mary J. Blige *No More Drama* (2001), Alicia Keys *Songs In A Minor* (2001).

PUNK ROCK

In the 70s punk was a massive sub-culture in the UK, created mainly out of a reaction to the hippy culture. It was heavily image based, Mohicans, piercings, safety-pins, skin tight trousers and the like. To match this image, punk rock music was loud, grinding and usually based around a very simple chord structure, with lyrics intended to shock and provoke a reaction.

THE SEX PISTOLS

America had its own punk scene, with bands such as The Velvet Underground, New York Dolls and Television leading the scene. Punk has had a massive influence on rock music, helping to create grunge rock in the 1990s, and more recently a new punk revival with bands such as The Libertines and The Others.

Listening Guide:
Sex Pistols *Never Mind The Bollocks Here's The Sex Pistols* (1977), The Stranglers *No More Heroes* (1977), The Clash *London Calling* (1979).

R 'N' B

Originally meaning Rhythm and Blues, this term has re-emerged over the last few years in a different guise, this time round describing a fusion of pop, soul and hip hop, primarily from the black culture.

Listening Guide:
Destiny's Child *Survivor* (2001), Craig David *Born To Do It* (2000), Justin Timberlake *Justified* (2003).

REGGAE
(Ska/Dub Reggae)

Jamaican popular music. Reggae has had an enormous influence on today's varied popular music culture, yet has been comparatively unsuccessful in terms of commercial success. Reggae is a blend of folk, jazz, rhythm and blues, African and Caribbean rhythms. Lyrically, the content was often politically tinged, and highly influenced by Rastafarianism. A result of reggae is **Ska**, which is slightly more hyper than reggae, and revived in the UK by bands like The Specials and Madness, who gave it commercial success.

Listening Guide:
Bob Marley & The Wailers *Legend* (1984 this is the best selling reggae album in the UK and the US), Lee 'Scratch' Perry *Arkology* (1997), The Trojan Club Reggae Box Set (2000), The Specials 'Ghost Town' (1981).

BOB MARLEY

TRANCE
(Goa/Psychedelic/Progressive/NU-NRG)
A form of electronic music combining techno and house music, primarily for clubs. The music is usually anthemic, with strong vocal or instrumental hooks over simple bass lines and a driving beat. Often highly synthesized, it is rich and powerful, classic uses of drop-outs of the beat or bass can create elation on the dance floor! The Ibiza club scene in the 90s was where trance music hit its peak.

Listening Guide:
BBE 'Seven Days And One Week' (1996), Energy 52 'Café Del Mar' (1997), Ayla 'Ayla' (1999), Motorcycle 'As The Rush Comes In' (2004).

TRIP-HOP
Pioneered mainly by Bristol group Massive Attack in the 90s, and followed by Portishead, the trip-hop style is a cool fusion of hip-hop beats, jazz, dub bass, atmospheric synths and ethereal vocals with a touch of soul and sometimes rap. Often trip-hop is recorded on lo-fi equipment, giving it a certain ambience.

191

PORTISHEAD

Listening Guide:
Massive Attack *Blue Lines* (1991), Portishead *Dummy* (1994), Tricky *Maxinquaye* (1994), Morcheeba *Big Calm* (1998).

WORLDBEAT (ETHNIC/WORLD)

Worldbeat is becoming more popular, and is even finding its way into the British charts in one way or another, most notably with the Asian music scene, led by bands such as Asian Dub Foundation and Panjabi MC. It is also becoming a popular club culture with pioneering DJs such as DJ Pathaan.

Often worldbeat music falls under the general 'world music' category, the only difference being the use of various mixes which make it suitable for clubs. An increasing amount of ethnic musicians are producing music that keeps their musical tradition whilst incorporating the Western style of beats.

Listening Guide:
Oi Va Voi *Laughter Through Tears* (2003), Nitin Sawhney *Beyond Skin* (1998), Sidestepper *More Grip* (2000), DJ Pathaan *Pathaan's Global Sunset* (2004).